UNDER THE
WEDDING CANOPY
Love and Marriage in Judaism

Other Books by David C. Gross

One Hundred Children by Lena Kuchler-Silberman,
  1961 (Translated from Hebrew)
The Hunter by Tuvia Friedman, 1962
  (Translated from Yiddish)
Dictionary of the Jewish Religion with Ben Isaacs, 1979
Hebrew Love Poems, 1995
A Treasury of Jewish Love, 1995

*   *   *

Updated
Pictorial History of the Jewish People by Nathan
  Ausubel, 1985

*   *   *

Pride of Our People, 1979
1,201 Questions and Answers About Judaism, 1980
The Jewish People's Almanac, 1981
A Justice for All the People: Louis D. Brandeis, 1987
How To Be Jewish, 1989
Hebrew-English/English-Hebrew Dictionary
  (Romanized), 1990
Laughing Through the Years, 1991
Judaism: A Religion of Deeds and Ideals, 1992
Jewish Wisdom (With Esther R. Gross), 1992
Yiddish-English/English-Yiddish Dictionary
  (Romanized), 1992
Why Remain Jewish?, 1994

UNDER THE WEDDING CANOPY
Love and Marriage in Judaism

David C. Gross
Esther R. Gross

Hippocrene Books
New York

For information, address:
HIPPOCRENE BOOKS, INC.
171 Madison Avenue
New York, NY 10016

Library of Congress Cataloging-in-Publication Data
Gross, David C., 1923-
   Under the wedding canopy : love and marriage in Judaism / David C.
Gross, Esther R. Gross.
    p.   cm.
   Includes bibliographical references and index.
   ISBN 0-7818-0481-7
   1. Marriage—Religious aspects—Judaism. 2. Marriage (Jewish law)
3. Marriage customs and rites, Jewish. 4. Jewish families -
-Religious life. I. Gross, Esther R. II. Title.
BM713.G78   1996
  296.4'44—dc20
                              96-28302
                                CIP

Printed in the United States of America.

For Marc and Robbin

God created the world in six days, the Bible notes. And on the seventh day, the Sabbath, He rested.
A sage asks: And what has He been doing since then? And a second sage replies: Matching up men and women, for marriage. For each marriage is like a new world.

* * *

The Baal Shem Tov, the founder of the Hassidic movement, taught: "From every human being there is a light that reaches to heaven. When two souls are destined to find each other, their streams of light fuse, and a single, brighter light goes forth from their united being."

Contents

PREFACE

Margaret Mead has written that "no matter how many communes anybody invents, the family always creeps back."

The family. We take it for granted, but think of it for a moment. A man and a woman fall in love; they get married and become loving companions, and in most cases a child or children follow in the course of time. And now we have a family, a whole new world in Jewish tradition.

As the husband and wife expand their roles into father and mother, and guide their offspring they come to realize—almost mystically—that in collaboration with God they have created a new human being... whom they will nurture, care for, and lead to adulthood.

In less turbulent times, families will lead a nation to peaceful goals; in turbulent times, families will band together to bolster each other and seek a return to happier days.

Anyone who thinks living together without benefit of marriage is a radical departure from stodgy old ways does not know his history. It has all been tried before and discarded, and then tried again and discarded again.

The family is the quintessential foundation stone of the world—and marriage is the foundation of the family. When you marry, you find a lifelong, loving, and devoted friend. You grow together, emotionally, spiritually, in all possible ways. There is no substitute for a happy marriage.

There are many *simchas*—joyous celebrations—in Judaism, and the greatest of them all is getting married. It is the *simcha* of *simchas*! If you are about to marry, or if you are married, we salute you and wish you joy and harmony.

–D.C.G., E.R.G.

CHAPTER ONE

The Jewish Concept of Marriage

In Genesis, the first volume of the Hebrew Bible, we are told: "Therefore shall a man leave his father and his mother, and shall cleave unto his wife, and they shall be one flesh."

Every year, for thousands of years of recorded history, men and women of every ethnic background, and of all religions, have reached out to each other and married. According to the Jewish mystical tradition, God is constantly creating new worlds—by causing marriages to take place.

Rabbi Daniel H. Gordis has written that the "relationship most approximating that between human beings and God is the marital relationship between a man and a woman." The biblical prophets, notably Hosea, described God's anger with the Jewish people—for having abandoned His teachings—as a messy divorce. Hosea exclaims: "She (the Jewish people) is not my wife and I am not her husband—And let her put away her harlotry from her face, and her adultery from between her breasts."

In a happy marriage, the rabbis taught, ideal human love is analogous to divine love. "If a man and wife are worthy, the Divine Presence is with them," notes the Talmud. "Whoever marries a worthy wife is kissed by Elijah and loved by the Holy One." Thus, a happy marriage, Judaism contends, is comparable to a happy, new world fashioned by God.

*   *   *

So, when you get right down to it, after nearly four thousand years of experience, just how does Judaism regard the idea of marriage? Simply stated, Judaism says that marriage is the ideal human condition and a basic social institution dating back to creation. It is said that when Adam and Eve were married, presumably in the Garden of Eden, God was their best man.

The Bible teaches that there are two principal purposes for marriage: Bringing children into the world and raising them, and companionship. "Be fruitful and multiply," we are instructed; and it is noted that "it is not good that a man should be alone," at which point God brings Eve into the world to be Adam's "helpmate."

Although a number of the famous biblical personalities had more than one wife, or a wife and a concubine, Judaism believed that marriage was a monogamous relationship. A careful reading of the Prophets and of the *Song of Songs* demonstrates clearly that monogamy is the ideal marital state. (Polygamy was banned among Ashkenazic Jews more than one thousand years ago; only the Yemenite Jews, isolated from world Jewry, who arrived in Israel more than forty years ago, still had more than one wife. As in virtually all modern societies, Israeli law prohibits polygamy.)

A careful reading of the Hebrew Bible will reveal that

in biblical times most marriages were arranged by the young couple's parents. Certain marital unions between close relatives were banned in biblical times, and are still forbidden. In biblical times every effort was made to assure a marriage within the Jewish community. The main fear in those days was that marrying out would unite a Jew with an idolater, and would weaken Judaism's resolve to maintain its distinctive character.

Judaism has always had an open, honest attitude towards the sexual side of marriage. The Bible speaks of Isaac "sporting" with Rebecca. Jacob, who labored a total of fourteen years before he could marry Rachel, says to his father-in-law, Laban: "Give me my wife...that I may go into her." Some rabbinical commentators were embarrassed by the directness of Jacob's words.

Perhaps Judaism's approach to marriage is best expressed by Ecclesiastes who advises: "Enjoy happiness with a woman you love all the days of life that have been granted to you under the sun—all your fleeting days. For that alone is what you can get out of life." Later, the rabbis taught that a man without a wife "exists without joy, without blessing or boon." The (Jerusalem) Talmud, reflecting the traditional Jewish view that marriage is analogous to God's relationship with humanity, states that a "man cannot live without a woman, and a woman cannot live without a man, and the two of them cannot live without the presence of God."

One other aspect of Jewish teaching about marriage is that it is a holy, sacred relationship entered into willingly by two adults. The Hebrew word for holy is *kadosh* which is allied to the Hebrew word for marriage, *kiddushin*.

*   *   *

If you pore through the Hebrew Bible carefully, you will

not find a straightforward description of a Jewish marriage ceremony as we know it today. There are however many biblical roots and hints of the modern Jewish wedding. The Jewish marriage customs and rituals stem from the two thousand-year-old teachings of the rabbinic period.

The biblical wedding ceremony which presumably existed in the marriages of those ancient times are described tersely. Either the groom *kidesh* the bride or *lakach* her. The former verb means he sanctified her, or set her aside; the latter verb means he took her. In Deuteronomy the groom is said to have taken and possessed her.

The celebration of Jacob's and Leah's wedding hints at a ceremony somewhat akin to Jewish weddings today, but there is no clear description. The importance of a bride's virginity is hinted at in various biblical references; to this day there are still a minuscule number of Jews among certain extremely Orthodox groups who place great stock in the bride's virginity, which must be proven after the wedding ceremony by displaying a bloody bedsheet.

Until the emancipation of the Jews in Europe, which began some two hundred years ago, the matchmaker (*shadchan*) was an important member of the community. He knew who was eligible to get married, and if he did his job right, he tried to unite couples with similar social and religious backgrounds. Nowadays most young Jews mock the very idea of a matchmaker, and seek to meet a suitable marriage partner in school, at work and at various social venues. There are however single's dances, or vacation sites dedicated to unmarried young individuals where people meet and sometimes have a happy marriage as a result.

In ancient times unmarried young women would don white gowns and twice a year present themselves to any eligible men. If a bachelor approached one of these would-be brides and indicated he would like to marry her, but she on the other hand was totally disinterested, he would have to keep looking. The idea of marrying for "love," was little-known until modern times. One can almost hear a would-be bride who lacked Elizabeth Taylor's looks many centuries ago saying to an eligible bachelor, "Remember the book of Proverbs: 'Charm is deceitful and beauty is vain, but a woman who fears the Lord will be praised.'"

* * *

As mentioned earlier, Judaism regards marriage as the ideal state. Indeed the rabbis taught that celibacy was unnatural. Unmarried man, they said, is a sinner for he "spends all his days in sinful thoughts." The Talmud said "he who has no wife is not a proper man." Sexual desire, Judaism teaches, is not evil when it is controlled and regulated in marriage. In fact, were it not for the *yetzer ha'ra* (evil inclination), "no man would build a house, marry a wife, or beget children." The rabbis said that to make a successful marriage is as hard as splitting the Red Sea. The Talmud even advises, "hurry to buy land but deliberate before taking a wife."

When a couple decides to marry, after they have ascertained that there are no legal barriers to their union (such as marrying a close relative, e.g., a step-sibling, or a wife's sister), the next step is to meet with a rabbi and discuss wedding plans. There are quite a few periods during the Jewish calendar year when marriages are not permitted (although the Reform branch of Judaism is much more lax about these restrictions).

After a date has been agreed upon, the site of the wedding must be determined. Jewish wedding ceremonies nowadays are held in synagogues, catering halls or hotels, in private homes, and occasionally in a park or at the beach. Strictly Orthodox couples often try to arrange for the ceremony to be held on a roof, under the open skies.

In the United States, in the late 1990s, half of all the marriages in which Jews take part, as either the groom or the bride, are with non-Jewish partners. Orthodox and Conservative rabbis will not officiate at such a wedding. Not all Reform rabbis will, but a growing number do. Their rationale is that they are reaching out to the non-Jewish partner in an effort to bring that person closer to Judaism, and eventually to formally convert and become Jewish. A smaller number of Reform rabbis will co-officiate at an intermarriage with a non-Jewish clergyman. Intermarried couples who can and do, choose to marry without any religious ceremony at all.

In the United States, marriages are performed according to the laws of the state in which they are held. Thus, there are states that ban unions between first cousins, and couples have been known to cross a state border in order to circumvent this law. (By and large Judaism permits such unions but rabbis must of course adhere to the laws of the individual state in which they officiate.)

The concept of marriage in Judaism is simultaneously simple and complex—simple because if two people are in love, have gotten to know each other during a reasonable period of courtship, and have concluded that they wish to spend their lives together and raise a family together, then nothing could be easier than standing under the traditional *chupah* (the wedding canopy) together with one's parents, close friends and relatives, and going through the relatively simple ceremonies that will change their status from a single person to a marriage partner.

And yet, it is also a complex step: the bride and the

groom who had hitherto been engaged, now become husband and wife, their lives intertwine from this point on; if they are blessed they produce a child or children, raise those little people to adulthood, and then, years later, become the parents escorting their offspring to the wedding canopy.

Not only are your bank accounts merged, but your outlook on life becomes "we" not "I" and you begin to realize that you are truly a nucleus of the whole world, very much a part of the universe but at the same time very much separate and apart from it.

Marriage, in other words, is the oldest human institution, the very foundation of civilization's most important cornerstone—the family.

The late Rabbi Aryeh Kaplan wrote: "The family has always been the strength of Judaism. Indeed, Judaism may be able to survive without the synagogue, but it cannot survive without the family. The foundation for the Jewish family is the Jewish wedding which sets the tone for the couple's future Jewish life." Or as Rabbi Pinchas Stolper has written, "the Jewish family is not a partnership, it is a merger," of two individuals, with two minds and personalities and characteristics and genes. In other words the "merger" (marriage) will not be easy to achieve but when the family is established it is at least twice as strong as before the wedding.

When the bride and groom stand under the wedding canopy and repeat the ritual phrases, they must remember that they have taken a step closer to holiness. They have become consecrated to each other. Two souls become fused into one family, an everlasting entity, destined to share each other's future. The rabbis of old described the wedding ceremony as leading to the creation of a home that in effect will become a small sanctuary.

Conjugal fidelity, Judaism teaches, is a *sine qua non* for

the new couple; a whole literature of laws and traditions grew over a period of many centuries to assure the bolstering of the Jewish family, and thus the well-being of the Jewish people.

Although the number of young people living together nowadays without benefit of the marriage ceremony continues to rise, the number of young couples anxious to get married in the traditional manner also continues to grow. As Rabbi Stolper writes: "The Jewish family has long been a model of harmony, love and stability, the envy of the entire civilized world. The very social evils that tend to disrupt and destroy modern society, such as divorce, prostitution, adultery, wife-beating or juvenile delinquency, were, until recent times almost unknown among traditional, unassimilated Jews. While observant Jews in America...have also been affected by this generation's tendency to solve marital problems through divorce, the difference in percentages still points to a qualitative difference of considerable weight."

* * *

The concept of the Jewish marriage is one that requires some study and understanding. It is hoped that by a deeper appreciation of the history and customs and traditions of the Jewish marriage through the centuries, young couples will approach their wedding day with reverence and joy, and embark on a long lifetime of holiness, fulfillment and happiness.

Chapter Two

How to Achieve Marital Happiness

"As long as they're happy!"

Who has not heard parents, siblings and friends lament a couple that is not married but live together for years, ignoring the wedding vows, flaunting society, doing "their own thing"?

It is interesting to note what Judaism has to say about happiness. What exactly is meant by that term? When do you know if you're happy? As it turns out, these are not new questions that have arisen in the latter part of the twentieth century—thoughtful people have asked these same questions for centuries.

The biblical Hebrew word for "happy" is *ashray*. Thus in Proverbs, we are taught that people who support the "tree of life" (wisdom) are happy. People who trust in God are happy, Psalms teaches. The teachings of Psalms declare that he who does not sin is happy, neither is the person who does not associate with sinful people. We are also taught (again in Psalms) that people who fear God are happy, or people who are compassionate towards the poor are happy. The great prophet Isaiah taught that people who keep the Sabbath—who hallow the day and transform it into a spiritual experience—are happy. And finally, Psalms advises that he who earns his livelihood by honest work, he too is happy.

What of the married couple? Obviously, all of the above applies to husband and wife, all the days of their lives. But there is more: for them loyalty to each other, compassion for each partner, considerateness, sexual fidelity, the raising of children in an atmosphere of love and caring, all these—and more—are conducive to a state of happiness.

"Do not call your wife 'wife,'" the rabbis taught. "Call her 'my home.'"

As the great Rabbi Akiba taught, "Who is rich? He who has a wife beautiful in deeds."

On the other hand, the Bible and the rabbinical commentators did not shy away from telling the stark, painful truth when they saw it. There are some wives, quite frankly, who are shrews. Proverbs states quite plainly that "it is better to dwell in a corner of the attic than in a house with a contentious woman." And a talmudic aphorism notes: "Better any ill or cruel fate than a cruel mate."

The German Jewish poet Heine would stand up and offer a toast at a suitable occasion. "Here's to marriage," he would say, "the great sea for which no compass has ever been invented." And the American playwright, Clifford Odets, in his famous play, "Golden Boy," wrote that "marriage is something special—I guess you have to deserve it."

*   *   *

Students of the Bible often point out that Abraham the

patriarch, King David, King Solomon, and other biblical personalities, practiced polygamy, if not always with full-fledged wives, then with concubines. Polygamy has been outlawed officially among Jews for more than one thousand years. And of the 2,000 rabbis who are mentioned in the Talmud, not one is listed as having more than one wife.

As Abraham ibn Ezra, the medieval poet and philosopher who lived in Spain, said, "One wife is enough for any man."

Traditionally, Jews are taught that the age of marriage is eighteen. Realistically, however, only among the strictly orthodox is this teaching still observed. However, the Talmud does teach: "First study, then marry; but if you cannot live without a wife, reverse the order."

Among very orthodox Jews it is not so unusual for a young couple to marry with the understanding that the young wife will earn a living while her husband spends several years, full-time, studying Jewish texts. Often by the time he is ready to go to work, his wife has already borne two or more children.

This arrangement is not very different from less religious couples, who marry with the understanding that the husband will continue his graduate studies in medicine or law or the sciences, while the wife works and in effect enables him to become a professional. Unfortunately, this system does not always work out. In the case of the orthodox couple, the husband usually studies in a "kollel" religious school, surrounded by other young husbands like himself. In the case of the non-religious couple, the husband is often surrounded by fellow female students. What often happens is that after he has obtained his graduate degree and begins to work as a physician or lawyer, he dumps his original wife, and marries someone he met in school.

*   *   *

How do you attain happiness, and build a happy marriage? A Yiddish proverb teaches, "Give your ear to all, your hand to friends, and your lips only to your wife." On the other hand, another Yiddish proverb reminds a husband: "A wife exults her husband, and a wife can cast him down."

To understand Jewish marriages today, one must remember that it is only two hundred years since Jewish families have accepted the notion that "love and marriage go together like a horse and carriage." Until that time, when by and large the political liberation of the Jews began to take place, the accepted system for betrothals was for fathers to arrange for their children's future spouses. A father generally looked for a respectable family, preferably with scholarly lineage, and if they were financially well-off, so much the better; if the girl or the young man were considered handsome, that too was a plus. Apparently most of these arranged matches worked out, divorce was a rarity in the pre-emancipation era begun by Napoleon.

And yet, over the years, Jews regarded marriages with a great range of viewpoints. In this they were not very different from their non-Jewish neighbors who also evolved both cynical and laudatory attitudes towards marriage.

Consider the Yiddish proverbs that have come down to us in the last few centuries:

When a young man marries, he "divorces" his mother.

The husband who marries for money—he earns it.

Even a mismatched married couple can have great children.

When two sleep on the same pillow, a third person may not intervene.

A couple might fight during the day, but at night they sleep together.

Between husband and wife, only God can judge.

The wedding ceremony lasts an hour but the troubles can endure a lifetime.

Marry in a hurry, and get stuck forever.

If a man who is married is tight with his money, he is hoarding money for his wife's next husband.

It is better to break an engagement than a marriage.

Marriage is made in heaven; a second marriage is arranged by people.

Nowadays young couples embarking on the marital sea tell their parents and friends that they "are in love." Jewish sages, especially those of our own time, regard such statements with a high degree of doubtfulness. A Yiddish proverb observes that "for a little love, you pay all your life." The Talmud teaches that "a woman prefers poverty with love to wealth without love." And the Bible cautions that "love is as strong as death." The great medieval Spanish Jewish poet, Shlomo ibn Gabirol, cautioned, "All love is real except that of the stupid."

In other words, marriage can be beautiful but you must think clearly before you decide to step under the wedding canopy and say "you are consecrated...."

Chapter Three

The Two-Part Wedding Ceremony

Jewish tradition, and indeed Jewish law, maintain that marriage is the ideal state. A Jew who deliberately abstains from getting married is regarded as a person who goes against Jewish religious law, including the first biblical commandment: "Be fruitful and multiply."

When a man dies and his soul moves to the next world, we are told, he will be asked: "Did you marry? How many children did you have?" And a man without a wife is not considered to be a full-fledged man—"he is without blessing, joy and goodness."

Halachah, Jewish religious law, specifically forbids marriage between siblings, a nephew and his aunt, and of course with parents or step-parents. On the other hand, an uncle may wed his niece, and the marriage of first cousins is permissible. A man may not marry his wife's sister as long as the wife is living.

There are other restrictions. Jews are classified according to lineage, dating back to the period of the Holy Temple. The *kohen* is a priest, and he is not allowed to marry a divorcee. (The rationale here is that the *kohen*—despite the fact that a Holy Temple has not stood in Jerusalem for 2,000 years—is still held to a higher level of observance than other Jews.)

Nowadays Jews of all groups, in every part of the world, adhere to monogamy. The only time a man may have two wives is when his first wife loses her mind, and is therefore considered unable to accept the husband's *get* (religious divorce). Under those circumstances, if the husband can get one hundred rabbis to sign a document permitting him to marry anew while his first wife is presumably confined to a mental institution, he can wed.

* * *

When a Jewish couple, unencumbered by any legal restrictions, decides to marry, what does the typical wedding ceremony consist of?

The actual ceremony usually lasts about a half-hour, with four men holding aloft the poles of the *chupah* (the wedding canopy), although sometimes the canopy is already fixed in place. (And at some feminist-oriented weddings, it is quite possible that women will carry the *chupah* aloft.)

The ceremony is a combination of *kiddushin* (sometimes also called *erusin*) and *nisu'in*. In ancient times, a year elapsed between both rites, so that the groom could go about preparing a home for the bride.

The first term (*kiddushin*) translates as "hallowing," i.e., the groom sanctifies the bride to be his wife. As was explained earlier, the term also connotes an act of holiness, for marriage is seen as a step towards a holy life. The principal part of the wedding ceremony occurs when the groom hands the bride a gold ring, in the presence of two reliable witnesses, and of the bride's accepting the ring—a sign that she agrees to be his wife. Under the terms of the *kiddushin* part of the rite, the couple is now formally, legally married and may have marital relations, as husband and wife. (In ancient times, between the two ceremonies the couple generally had to wait a whole year for consummation).

The bride and groom, before the ring ceremony, led by the officiating rabbi, recite two blessings and sip some wine. Then the groom places the ring on the bride's right forefinger, reciting in Hebrew: "You are consecrated unto me with this ring according to the laws of Moses and Israel."

At this point the rabbi will read aloud the *ketubah* (the marriage contract), which is in Aramaic, the lingua franca of ancient Israel. Some rabbis will read the entire document, and some will skim the highlights, usually adhering to the wishes of the family. The ring ceremony is followed by a separate cup of wine, over which seven blessings are recited (of which six deal with the wedding). Then follows the groom stomping on an empty glass, breaking it as a remembrance of the Temple that was destroyed in Jerusalem two millennia ago. This signals the assembled guests to applaud and cheer as the couple, now legally wed, embrace and kiss.

The *chupah* can be cloth embroidered and decorated, or it can even be a large *tallit* (a prayer shawl). It is customary for the groom to wait under the *chupah* while his bride enters—symbolizing that this is the groom's home, and she willingly enters it to become his wife.

The *ketubah*, the marriage contract, can be a simple printed sheet of paper or an artistically designed work of art attesting to the fact that the groom agrees to support his wife during their marriage, and to pay for her upkeep if the marriage ends in divorce, or if the groom dies.

One of the reasons for the *ketubah* is the fact that under

Jewish law a husband can divorce his wife rather easily—
he need merely hand her a *get* (a religious divorce document), and if he needs a reason he can claim she burned
the food she prepared for him. Thus, for the wife's protection from such behavior, the marriage contract was
instituted, whereby a divorce requires the husband to
provide substantially for his wife.

At some very Orthodox weddings the groom may be
seen wearing a *kittel* (a white gown) over his clothes
during the wedding ceremony. The tradition for this is
very simple: on Yom Kippur, the Day of Atonement, very
observant Jewish men wear a kittel over their clothes
during the day they spend in the synagogue. The white
gown symbolizes purity, and just as the worshiper on Yom
Kippur approaches his prayers with a sense of purity, the
groom sees his new life as a husband as the beginning of
a new life for himself, and begins it dressed in a pure,
white gown.

Many Jewish couples, both bride and groom, also fast
on the day of their wedding, reminiscent of the fast on
Yom Kippur.

It is also customary for the groom to be called to the
Torah for Sabbath services on the Saturday before his
wedding. This practice is known as an *ofruf*, a calling-up,
and is usually an opportunity for the parents of both bride
and groom and their guests to participate in the service.
Usually the soon-to-be-wed couple's parents (and even
more often the bride's parents) host a festive meal after
the *ofruf* for their guests. This custom is quite widespread
among Ashkenazic Jews, but among Sephardic Jews the
ofruf and the festive meal take place after the wedding
ceremony.

Among Orthodox Jews the bride does not take part in
the calling-up ceremony, since she and the groom traditionally do not see one another for a week before the

wedding. Among Conservative and Reform Jews, who form the majority of American and western Jews, particularly in a synagogue that follows the egalitarian service, not only is the bride in attendance at the *ofruf* ceremony, but many times she joins her future husband when he is called up to the Torah. Generally the officiating rabbi at that point in the ceremony will extend the congregation's greetings to the couple and present the bride and groom with a synagogue gift.

*   *   *

There are other ceremonies associated with the Jewish wedding but not all rabbis encourage them. Mostly, they are followed in the Orthodox community but some are also adhered to among Conservative and sometimes Reform Jews. For example, before the wedding ceremony the bride sits in a decorated chair, festooned with flowers; sometimes she is isolated in a small room outside the main wedding hall, and sometimes she sits in the principal reception room. Just prior to the wedding ceremony, the groom approaches her, usually accompanied by a few musicians and some of his ushers, and ceremoniously covers his future wife's face with a decorated veil. This is known as the *badecken*, a Yiddish term meaning "covering up" and is reminiscent of the biblical account—when Rebecca saw Isaac, her future husband, she covered her face.

Some Orthodox wedding ceremonies include the bride's walking around her husband-to-be seven (sometimes only three) times. This aspect of the wedding rite recalls a phrase in the biblical book of Jeremiah where the ancient prophet proclaims that a "woman shall go around a man." There are those who offer another explanation:

from that point on, the bride will regard her husband as the center of her life.

In the United States and most western countries the groom is escorted to the *chupah* by his parents, and then the bride is brought halfway down the aisle by her parents, after which the groom walks back along the aisle and escorts her the rest of the way to the wedding canopy. In Israel, and in some Sephardic communities, the groom is escorted by the two fathers and the bride by the mothers.

At Hasidic weddings, the entertainment provided for the benefit of the new couple often includes juggling acts, aerobatics, and flamboyant dancing. The reason for this is the talmudic dictum that it is a *mitzvah*, a good deed, to make the bride and groom happy at their wedding. The famous Rabbi Hillel taught, millennia ago, that a bride must be described to the groom as "beautiful and charming" even though she might not be.

Traditional Jewish couples will depart from their wedding for a honeymoon, during which it is customary for them to eat at least one festive meal in a public place, where a quorum of at least ten men join them in singing the "seven blessings" (*sheva b'rachot*) as part of the grace that is recited after a meal. It is also customary for the men at the table to include at least one person who was not in attendance at the wedding.

As the young couple enter upon the uncharted sea of marriage, the new husband is cautioned by Jewish law that he is required to furnish his wife with three basic provisions: food, clothing, and satisfaction of her sexual needs. Through this teaching, Judaism demonstrates that it regards marital sex as an instrument not only for procreation but also for enjoyment and an ever-closer bond between man and wife. If a wife is barren, or on the contrary, if she is pregnant, the husband is still required to fulfill her sexual needs. It is only during a woman's menstrual period, when she is regarded as temporarily "impure," that marital relations are proscribed.

Rabbi Norman Lamm, the president of Yeshiva University, in his delightful book, *A Hedge of Roses*, offers the romantic explanation that the enforced monthly period of abstinence actually makes the monthly resumptions of relations seem like a renewed honeymoon.

As is generally known, Jewish wives are required by law to immerse themselves in a *mikvah* for ritual purification after the end of their monthly period, and although many women no longer adhere to this teaching, hundreds of thousands still do. Interestingly, Jews are taught that when they enter a new geographical area, the first community building they put up should not be a synagogue or a school but a *mikvah*.

*   *   *

In our day and age, when more than half of the newly-married couples are likely, according to the latest statistical data, to get divorced, the question that must be confronted realistically is: How difficult is it to obtain a *get*? In actuality it is quite simple—but only if husband and wife both agree that they want it, and if there are no bitter arguments about who gets to keep the children, visitation rights, property settlements, and the like. In such cases it often gets acrimonious.

If both husband and wife agree to divorce, they must ask a *sofer* (a scribe) to write out a *get* with all the details of the separation spelled out; the husband then hands the handwritten document to his wife and the painful process is begun. Of course, the husband must prove that he fulfilled all that he promised in the *ketubah*. And if the wife does not want the divorce, he can't force her. In recent years there are increasing reports of husbands who refuse to grant their wives a *get*—unless they are paid a substantial amount of money. Religious Jewish women will not, and often cannot, remarry without a *get* even though they may have a perfectly valid civil divorce.

Orthodox and Conservative rabbis basically will not officiate at a remarriage of a previously married man or a woman who lacks a *get*. There have been sad cases of men who abandoned their wives and children, leaving the wife in a state of limbo. She is unable to proceed with her life until she is legally and formally divorced from her ex-husband. In most of these instances, the husband demands exorbitant sums; at times he is just being spiteful, and sometimes he disappears without leaving a trace, creating a serious problem for the wife. Such a woman is known as an *agunah*, "an achored one," for without a *get* she is still anchored to her ex.

Although a civil divorce can be obtained by couples that split up, it is not recognized in Jewish law. This means that although a couple may think they are divorced, having obtained a civil divorce, yet fail to obtain a *get*, and then the woman remarries, Jewish law regards her—in her new marriage—as adulterous. Any children born in such a marriage are looked upon, in Jewish law, as bastards (*mamzerim*), forbidden to marry a fellow Jew although they may marry a fellow *mamzer*.

To prevent the tragedy of the *agunah*, married Israeli soldiers are required to sign a document stating that if they are lost in action for a certain period of time (usually five years), they may be declared dead, and their wives would then be free to remarry.

Reform rabbis generally officiate at marriages of people who have only a civil divorce, a practice that exacerbates the chasm between Reform Jews and the Orthodox and Conservative communities.

Chapter Four

Married Life Can Be Beautiful, Or Painful

Marriage can be beautiful, a veritable bed of roses, a source of unending joy. Unfortunately, it can also be a source of pain and trouble.

There are young couples who marry, and after a few months or years they decide to expand their family and have children. They throw out all their birth control devices, and depend on nature to add a new dimension to their lives.

Months pass, and nothing happens. They visit a doctor to discuss their problem, and more often than not they will be referred to a fertility specialist. Blood tests are taken, as are other tests.

The results come back: he is infertile, or she is infertile. It takes time to absorb this and to cope with it. Because there is genuine love and respect between husband and wife, they calmly talk over their options. They can adopt; they can take advantage of the new, in vitro methods of fertilizing the wife's egg, either with the husband's sperm, or with that of a total stranger. Or, of course, they can opt to go through life childless, a condition designated a tragedy by the Bible.

Adopting and raising a child in Jewish tradition is tantamount to being that child's biological parent. Many childless Jewish couples have adopted children of various ethnic backgrounds and raised them in the Jewish faith; in the vast majority of cases, both the parents and the adopted children have voiced joy and satisfaction from their decision to take what is admittedly a difficult step.

In our own family a young cousin who was unable to conceive adopted a Chinese infant girl. According to Jewish religious law she had to be converted; the brief ceremony was conducted by a rabbi, using a *mikvah* for the venue. The little girl was given the name of Sarah and a middle name of Hannah, in memory of the adoptive grandfather's sisters, who died in the Holocaust.

Once a child is converted to the Jewish faith, the child is regarded as Jewish in every sense. If, for example, one of the adoptive parents should die, the child is expected to recite the mourner's *kaddish* prayer for the parent, just as if he/she were a biological parent.

In our own synagogue we have a young man, a Korean, a physician, who converted to Judaism prior to marrying the daughter of one of the member families. In the course of the conversion process, he mastered Hebrew, and whenever he is in synagogue on the Sabbath and is called to the Torah, he is summoned by his new Hebrew name, Shmuel. When he recites the appropriate blessings before his section of the Torah reading, most members of the congregation come up with the same observation: He knows the blessings better than some of the born Jews.

* * *

In vitro, as a method of aiding a couple to have a child, poses a more difficult problem. There are basically two types of artificial insemiation: AIH, where the husband is the doner of the sperm, and AID, where the donor is someone other than the husband. The morality of injecting a stranger's sperm into a woman not his wife, even without any sexual intercourse between the two, has been debated among rabbis for many years. Most rabbinical authorities sanction the husband being the donor in an artificial insemination situation.

It is when the donor is a stranger that serious ethical problems arise for the rabbinical authorities. In addition to the problem of ethics, some rabbis worry deeply about the possibility of incest at some point in the future. The argument goes like this: If the unknown donor, years later, has a child with his wife, and that child somehow meets and marries the child whom he helped to bring into the world, such a marriage would be a clear case of incest.

Some rabbis also contend that the notion of a married woman becoming impregnated with a stranger's semen, even without sexual intercourse, is an unsavory action. Oddly, if a single young woman becomes pregnant through a donor's sperm under the same circumstances, some rabbis do not react quite the same way.

When you come right down to it, with the exception of the Orthodox community, artificial insemination becomes a matter for a personal decision. By and large Orthodox Jews tend to adhere to the rules and regulations laid down by *Halachah*, Jewish religious law, and their own rabbis' interpretations. Reform and Conservative Jews on the other hand, as well as their rabbis in many cases, take a less stringent view, hoping that their decision to insemi-nate the wife with a stranger's sperm will work out.

Another objection raised by some against a stranger's sperm is that if the child ever turns ill, chances are very slim that the parents will ever be able to learn if the child inherited a tendency to a particular disease.

* * *

How many children should a Jewish couple aim for? Most rabbis seem to be of the opinion, following the biblical injunction that we should "be fruitful and multiply," that the more the merrier. Among Orthodox Jews there is an unspoken feeling that in the wake of the Holocaust, when one-third of the Jewish people were wiped out, we should have as many children as we can. This explains, in part, the large number of children usually found in their families.

From the Orthodox viewpoint, it is also sinful to "waste seed" when having intercourse. Those Orthodox Jews who do have smaller numbers of children generally use the pill, believing that this method of birth control somehow is less wasteful of seed. Conservative and Reform rabbis by and large allow their congregants to decide for themselves how many children they want, how they are to be spaced in the family, and what methods of birth control they choose.

* * *

In the final years of the twentieth century it seems sometimes that homosexuality and lesbianism have grown in popularity. Those who live in this sector of society insist that ten percent of the population is essentially gay, but most scientific data indicate that this lifestyle is confined to no more than one or perhaps two percent of the American population. Still, in the United States with close to 265 million, one percent means more than two and a half million are gay—quite a large number.

There is also a perception that there are a lot of Jews in

this group, although no one has ever found any scientific evidence. Many people have heard eligible young Jewish girls who would like to get married complain about Jewish young men that they're "either married, mama's boys, or gay."

The Bible of course teaches that there is nothing new under the sun. Ergo, one should not be surprised to learn that millennia ago there were, apparently, men who tended toward homosexuality and women who leaned in the direction of lesbianism. The Bible, as the great teacher of morality, warns that if a man "lie with a man, as with a woman, it is an abomination," and both men should be put to death. Women were also cautioned not to emulate "the doings after the land of Egypt, where you dwelled" but they are not threatened with a penalty of death. The Talmud states however that if a woman performs a sexual act with another woman, the two of them will no longer be regarded as virgins. Why Judaism is more lenient toward women is not clear. Interestingly, the talmudic sages never designated either homosexuals or lesbians as separate groups, but merely spoke of men or women having homosexual natures or inclinations.

In Judaism the concept of love is primarily used for expressing one's devotion to God and people, as in the well-known phrase that adorns many synagogues, "Love your neighbor as yourself."

When it comes to expressing a man's love for a woman, or vice versa, it seems that suddenly Jews in days of old turned shy. Or to put it another way, the love that a Jewish couple feels for one another should be voiced first and foremost through deeds rather than talk. Also, there is a perception in Judaism that marriage should be for the long haul; perhaps there is a fear that one should not talk of love between husband and wife until they have lived happily together for many years. Only then is it seemly to speak of marital love.

One rabbi comments on the biblical verse describing Rebecca's arrival in Isaac's home. The Bible says: "Isaac brought her into his mother Sarah's tent, and took Rebecca, and she became his wife, and he loved her." It is the order that intrigues this rabbinical commentator: First, she became his wife, and then he loved her. In other words, the deep love that Isaac felt for her continued on long after the wedding, which is as it should be, for in all too many sad cases first comes love, then marriage, and all too often—for whatever reason—a divorce.

As the Yiddish proverb teaches: "Love me a little less, but longer."

Jewish tradition is one hundred percent for marriage, and believes strongly that after a period of time a married couple will grow together and remain in love forever. Who can forget that marvelous line in *Fiddler on the Roof* when Tevya asks his wife, "Do you love me?" And she looks at him as though he has gone mad. "Do I WHAT?" she asks, and then begins to sing about the meals she cooks for him, the laundry she does, the children she bore. That, she makes crystal clear, is love.

* * *

Some newlywed Jewish couples sometimes ask how is it possible that in biblical times polygamy not only was permitted but some of the great figures mentioned in the Bible—Abraham, Jacob, King David, Solomon—all had multiple wives, or at least one wife and openly accepted concubines.

The fact is that polygamy has been banned among Jews for more than one thousand years. In addition, of the 2,000 rabbis mentioned in the various tractate of the Talmud, not one practiced polygamy. In ancient times, it was explained, a woman alone without the protection of a husband was in danger, while a man alone was not. Thus, bringing another woman into the home was an act of kindness.

A careful reading of the Bible demonstrates that monogamy was, even in those days, looked upon as the ideal state. The famous quotation in the book of Proverbs about a "woman of valor" speaks about one woman, no women. In the prophetic book of Hosea, there is a metaphor of God's love for the Jewish people and the Jewish people's love for God—this love is described as the love between husband and wife. And of course, in the opening pages of the Bible we meet Adam and Eve, one man and one woman.

*   *   *

From its very beginnings, Judaism has always had a straightforward attitude toward sex in marriage. When Eve arrives, the Bible states very clearly that a "man shall leave his father and his mother, and shall cleave unto his wife, and they shall be one flesh." All the patriarchs, as well as Moses, and the various biblical heroes marry and have children. Never is there a hint that the holiness of these individuals is compromised or reduced because they have wives and children. A man is not considered a man, the Talmud teaches, unless he marries and has children. The Song of Songs is a magnificent song of praise to love and to physical sex. In Genesis, Isaac is described as "sporting" with Rebecca—just like any young couple.

If there was a flip side to this situation, it was that the ancient rabbis had little if any opportunity to carry on social contact with women other than their wives. According to C.G. Montefiore, "social intercourse with women was usually taboo." Women were seen as the "source of moral danger... and incitements to depravity and lust." Montefiore adds: "The rabbis were prevailingly chaste; there probably was much less adultery and fornication among them than among us...but the lack of healthy, simple companionship and friendship caused a constant dwelling upon sexual relations... immense are the Halachic discussions (in rabbinic literature) about the details of sex life."

No wonder that the talmudic rabbis taught: "Don't talk too much with women."

Chapter Five

When Two Merge—And Remain Two

People who have attended a Jewish wedding, both Jewish and non-Jewish guests, generally find the event both enjoyable and exhilarating.

When the bride and groom walk down the aisle, separately before the ceremony, and then arm in arm after they have been pronounced married, there is usually a happy ambience that wafts over the entire assemblage.

There are exceptions of course, as when the parents of either the bride or the groom really object to the marriage. Occasionally this results from the fact that the groom is much older then the bride, or perhaps because one of the two has been married frequently before, or they are both of different ethnic and/or religious backgrounds—and even though the non-Jewish partner in the marriage has converted to Judaism, sometimes there is a festering fear or suspicion that this was done for ulterior reasons: the bride is rich, or the groom is rich. This of course is not the best way to begin on the marital path.

But when the couple is deemed well-suited, from similar if not identical social, economic and educational backgrounds, and when it is obvious that they genuinely love one another, then the wedding ceremony and the reception that usually follows is a joyous celebration of life itself. No wonder so many people often exclaim, "I love to go to weddings!"

After all, what really happens here is the bride and groom willingly give up their singleness and agree to merge two lives together, to form in effect a new family, a new nucleus, from whence will come, it is hoped, children who in turn will carry on the family name, and in the course of time enable the bride and groom—through the children—to achieve a form of immortality. And all of this is done without philosophy and deliberateness, but rather with openly-expressed love, with music and dancing, and joy.

In a sense, getting married is like being born again. Both the bride and the groom are transformed into husband and wife, usually following in the footsteps of their parents and grandparents, and sometimes are amazed that they are taking this step which, in many cases, they mocked in their formative years. The first weeks and months, and even years, of marriage are a learning process. Whatever he does from this point on, he soon discovers, has to include consideration of his wife—a word and idea that takes some time to adjust. And she? She has the same situation to adjust: Will he like this kind of meal for dinner? Does he like a quiet dinner after a hectic day at work, or would he like to talk about something totally irrelevant?

Both husband and wife, slowly, gradually, learn what it is that the partner in the marriage likes or dislikes, and most of the time a serious effort to accommodate to the new circumstance is made. Thus, what actually happens is that in the first months and years of the marriage, both husband and wife without even realizing it change; whatever they do, whatever they plan, they find themselves including the marriage partner in the deliberations. Over a period of time their vocabulary changes from "I" to "we"—and they begin to realize that although in many ways they remain individuals, at one and the same time they have become fused into a couple, united, stronger than during the days of their singlehood, and prepared to confront the whole world from a completely different perspective. After all, their subconscious tells them, now you are married!

*   *   *

When a bride and groom who are observant of religious commandments are about to be married, they generally feel very close to the ceremonial ritual. The words that the rabbi pronounces, the blessings he offers them, all have a familiar ring, for the words are similar to blessings found in the daily and Sabbath prayerbook and in the holiday prayerbook.

And what is surprising is that even a non-religious bridal couple finds an echo in the words that are offered.

For example, when the groom, just prior to the actual wedding ceremony, approaches his bride and places the veil on her face (the *badeken*) and says to her, aloud for all to hear, "May you be fruitful and prosper. May God make you as Sarah, Rebecca, Rachel and Leah. May the Lord bless you and keep you. May the Lord show you favor and be gracious to you. May the Lord show you kindness and grant you peace." Even the least-educated couple in Judaism knows about the Matriarchs, and to be welcomed as a bride and compared to the Matriarchs at one's wedding sets the tone for the religious ceremony that is to follow, and hopefully for the entire marriage. In other words, both bride and groom up to that point may have been ultra-busy preparing for the wedding, and for the honeymoon, and for their new home—and now, with a few hallowed words, they come to realize that their union as husband and wife is to be a holy alliance.

When the two stand under the wedding canopy, surrounded by parents, siblings, and of course the rabbi (and sometimes a cantor) and drink from one cup of wine, reciting the blessing of thanks that accompanies this rite, they cannot help but feel that they are stepping into a new dimension. And when the groom gives a gold wedding band to his bride and says: "Behold, you are sanctified to me by this ring in accordance with the laws of Moses and Israel"—only the most insensitive couple will fail to realize that they have just linked themselves across time to a tradition and a heritage that is nearly four thousand years old.

Toward the end of the wedding ceremony, the last blessing offered to the newly-married couple voices the hope that "there will always be heard in the cities of Judah and in the streets of Jerusalem voices of joy and gladness, voices of the bride and groom, the joyous voices of those joined in marriage under the bridal canopy, the voices of young people feasting and singing."

This final benediction of the traditional seven blessings reflects the impassioned hopes of the prophet Jeremiah, who prophesied a new age for the Jewish people, when they would return from exile and redeem the country that had been laid waste.

There is a hint of the messianic era in every Jewish wedding ceremony, which regards the land of Israel as the bride and God Himself as the groom.

A wit once commented that although it is true that a newlywed couple has to experience fusion in their married years, more often than not—at least for a while—there is more confusion than fusion. Some commentators state that every Jewish couple that marries in a Jewish religious ceremony is like Adam and Eve: untested, unknowing, with a whole world waiting for them.

One can say that a Jewish wedding ceremony is like a replay of Jewish history and Jewish teaching. The new couple is connected to ancient days, to Patriarchs and Matriarchs, to hope and prayer. When the couple steps away from the wedding canopy, now married and proclaiming to the world that they are husband and wife, they have established themselves as a new link in the long chain of Jewish history. When the two of them depart for their honeymoon and new life, they are alone of course, but at the same time they are not alone. They are eternally connected to the Jewish people, past, present and future.

* * *

The fundamental importance of marriage in the Jewish community is emphasized again and again in the Talmud, in the Yiddish culture that flourished a few centuries ago in eastern Europe, and in many other Jewish sources. The Apocrypha quotes Ben Sira as teaching: "Without a hedge the vineyard is laid waste, and without a wife a man is a homeless wanderer. Who trusts an armed band of vagabonds?" The late Rabbi Barnett Brickner wrote that "happiness in marriage is not a gift but an opportunity. It is an obligation, not an experiment. The chief purpose of marriage is the making of a home, the rearing of children, and the (couple's) working together for economic security."

Of course there are the cynics, clever people who undoubtedly did not enjoy a happy, blissful marriage. Disraeli, who was baptized when he was a child, nevertheless always thought of himself as a Jew. He wrote: "I have always thought that every woman should marry, but no man."

*   *   *

There is no clear-cut description in the Bible of a Jewish wedding ceremony as we know it today. Nevertheless, there are strong hints in the Bible of the kind of celebration that accompanied a marriage. This is especially true in the story of Father Jacob and the most-beloved of his two wives and two concubines, namely Rachel. Even in the brief description of Jacob's marriage to Leah, into which he was tricked by his father-in-law Laban, there are indications that some sort of public, communal festivity accompanied the event. On the other hand, there is a biblical account of the marriage of Moses' parents in which it is declared starkly that Amram "took" Yocheved, and apparently that was it. Elsewhere in the Bible it states that "a man takes a wife and possesses her" and that apparently was the way it was done in those far off days.

We hear nowadays about a matchmaker, a *shadchan*, who brings eligible young men and women together for the purpose of marriage. In Europe, both in the more enlightened western countries and in eastern Europe, in the isolated regions of the small hamlets, the *shadchan* was a very important part of the community in the eighteenth and nineteenth centuries. Today, of course, there are lots of people who act as unofficial matchmakers—parents, friends, relatives, neighbors, who try to bring unmarried people together—but they do this out of a sense of caring or duty, not as a profession. Indeed, there is a Jewish tradition stating that if anyone has succeeded in arranging three marriages here on earth, then in the next world he/she is assured of entry into the Garden of Eden!

Actually, among the very Orthodox Jews the institution still exists, particularly among the Hasidic sects.

What happens often is that a young man, say in his very late teens or very early twenties, would like to continue his religious studies for a few years but cannot afford to be unemployed, then a friend, sometimes a rabbi, will speak to a father of a young woman and arrange a match, stressing the scholarly attributes of the potential groom. Then, what generally happens is the young lady—after the wedding—sets up house with her husband and goes to work, supporting the two of them while the husband attends a *kollel*, a school for advanced religious studies generally attended by young male adults, many of them married. Sometimes when the young couple begins to have children and the young wife finds that taking care of her family, including the husband, and holding down a job are all too much for her, she tells her husband, "Okay, that's it, now you go to work." Or words to that effect.

While these arranged marriages may seem at first blush cold, calculating affairs in which both husband and wife have little to say about choosing a lifetime partner, in reality they do. When unmarried, they do date, although often under the watchful eye of a chaperone-relative (we're speaking here of Hasidim and other ultra-Orthodox Jews). If either he or she finds the proposed mate distasteful or in any way unsuitable, they simply notify the parents that they do not wish to continue, and more often than not, the dating is ended. Even the Talmud, millennia ago, said clearly: "It is forbidden for a man to marry a woman until he sees her." Although romantic love as we know it in the twentieth century may seem to be underplayed among some Orthodox Jews, it is incorrect to say that it is completely swept away. All young Jewish couples, even the most traditional, insist on having a say in the matter of choosing a life partner.

*   *   *

It is important to remember in any discussion of Jewish marriage that Jewish tradition and teaching regard sexuality in marriage as a strong, positive drive in life. As has been noted earlier, a wife is required to receive from her husband three things: food, clothing and satisfaction of her sexual needs. There is a well-known discussion recorded in the Talmud between two of its most famous commentators-interpreters, Rabbi Shammai and Rabbi Hillel. The latter is always seen as gentle and lenient, and the former as stern and strict. A discussion between the two centers on the question of a husband's marital responsibilities, with Shammai saying that a recalcitrant husband has two weeks to fulfill his duties to his wife. Hillel maintains that such a husband has only one week, and if he fails to meet his wife's requirements, she can sue for divorce.

CHAPTER SIX

The Real Goal of Jewish Marriage
Is Holiness

In the early days of the Soviet Union, the western concept of marriage—based on the teachings of the Hebrew Bible—were denounced and ignored. And within a very short time, the Soviets reversed themselves and decreed that marriage was to be retained as a social institution that is the basis of the family, and that the family in turn is the basis of society as we know it today. Early experiments in polyandry—multiple husbands—were quickly condemned, and traditional marriage norms were quickly reinstated.

The laws of marriage, and the traditions and customs surrounding it, were not promulgated by ancient rabbis but rather evolved over a period of many centuries, through trial and error, through religious legislation, and through amendments to these laws as circumstances warranted. Way back then the rabbis and sages who devoted their time to interpreting and reinterpreting the Torah, and later the Talmud, came to realize—long before the word marriage was invented—that unless society followed certain stringent rules in marriage, human beings could easily slip into an Orwellian mode. It is certainly true that the rabbis of two thousand years ago were lacking our modern technology, and some would even say their lives, compared to ours, were primitive; nevertheless, they understood human nature, morality, human foibles and weaknesses and they succeeded in figuring out a way of teaching men and women how to live ethical lives that would result in truly happy and satisfying lives.

*   *   *

One of the great differences between Judaism and other religious faiths is the Jewish goal—in an individual, in a family, even in a whole community—of striving for holiness. The Bible teaches that God is holy, and also declares that God has made people in His image, and therefore all people must strive for holiness. This concept refers not only to prayer and formal worship but also directs the individual's attention to virtually every aspect of his/her daily life. Meals, work, play, study: all must be hallowed. As for marriage, how can there be any question about the holiness of this sacred institution, in which a man and a woman come together to merge their lives into one unit, to help one another, to have and raise children who will also follow a holy path, and by following these ancient laws and paths will sanctify their own lives and set an example for the next generation?

Matching up a man and a woman for marital purposes may at first seem pretty routine, until you try it. In American suburbia, it is told, Jewish parents anxious to see their children get married and settle down have found that if they make a direct effort to introduce their sons or daughters to someone suitable, it almost inevitably ends in arguments, rejections, and bad feelings. Ergo, what happens nowadays is that two sets of parents—friends of long standing—get together and decide that each set will work on the child of the other; after all they're friends, not parents, and introduce the unmarried young man or woman to someone they met, or heard of, and surprisingly sometimes this tactic works.

There is a talmudic tale of a Roman woman, when told that since creation of the world, God had been busy arranging matches, scoffed and said she also could do it. In the next few days, she paired off one thousand male slaves with one thousand slave girls, and felt very pleased with herself. Until the complaints began to come in! It seems that not one match was happy, at which point the Roman lady admitted that matchmaking was indeed a very awesome and difficult job, and that it had better be left to God in heaven.

The story of Jacob and Rachel, as told in the Bible, is as romantic a tale as they come. Poor Jacob: he had fallen deeply in love with Rachel, agreed with her father Laban to work seven years before he could marry her, and then was tricked by Laban to marry the other sister, Leah, and had to work an additional seven years. A less famous story displaying romantic love in Jewish tradition is one of the great Rabbi Akiva. In Jewish history he has remained one of the great sages, a leader and a fountain of profound learning, and yet, when he was still in his forties, he was completely illiterate, and therefore of course quite ignorant of Judaism and Jewish teaching.

Well, almost like the old movies, he meets a young lady named Rachel, they fall in love, her father disowns her for taking up with an ignorant shepherd, and then the wife makes what turns out to be a historic decision: She wants her husband to start learning, full-time, first the simple alphabet, and eventually the great texts of Judaism. And of course she will provide for him.

Circumstances are such that they are separated for many years, while she toils in one city and he studies far away in another. Gradually, Akiva gets to be known as a great rabbi and teacher, and after a separation of many years the two meet again and are reunited. And Akiva's name is added to the roster of outstanding Jewish scholars. (Today of course there are schools that bear Akiva's name).

The moral? Judaism has a healthy respect for romantic love, but it should be allied to a religious precept.

*   *   *

Marriage, Judaism teaches, is not to be taken lightly. If a man wishes to marry, and is lacking in funds, but owns a Scroll of the Law (a hand-inscribed Torah), he may sell it in order to get married. Marriage, we are told, should never be for money. A man should look for a woman who is gentle, modest, industrious, and tactful. Also, she should be beautiful, from a suitable social background, not too old nor too young, and whose father can be described as learned and scholarly. Further, a man should not plan to wed someone whom he does not know well.

A Yiddish wit comments on a man's marriage to a woman for the sake of money: "He'll find out he has to earn it!" And another notes that many a woman would rather have a bad marriage than be alone.

The sages and rabbis of the last two millennia developed a clear-cut approach to sexuality, which they regarded as a normal, healthful and important part of marriage. In giving students instruction how they should conduct themselves when they marry, they usually used euphemistic language, but did not hesitate to tackle the most difficult of problems. When, for example, they wished to say that a man should not have marital relations with his wife and think of another woman during the coital act, they said: "One should not drink from this glass, and cast his eyes upon another."

A talmudic tale is told of a young student about to marry who asked his rabbi to teach him about what he should do in the marital bed. The rabbi refused. A few nights later the rabbi discovered that his student was hiding under his bed. Flabbergasted, the rabbi asked what he was doing there. The student defended himself: "It is Torah, and I need to learn!"

The health-related aspects of a good sexual life were known to rabbis and sages many centuries ago. Sometime in the early part of the thirteenth century the great commentator Nahmanides, who had built a reputation as a strict legal expert, was said to have composed a prayer directed straight at God: "O my Lord, God and God of my fathers, ground of all the universes, for the sake of Your great and holy name alluded to in the verse 'The Lord has remembered us, He will bless the House of Israel, He will bless the House of Aaron,' may it be Your will that you emanate from Your spirit of power unto me and give me might and strength in my organs and my body that I might regularly fulfill the commandment pertaining to my sexual cycle; that there be not found in my organs, body or passion any weakness or slackness, that there be not forcing unseemly thought, confusion of mind, or weakening of power to prevent me from fulfilling my desire with my wife. Rather, now and forever, let my passion be ready for me without fail or slackness of organ, at any time that I should desire, Amen."

Judaism is opposed to adultery, of course. It is one of the Ten Commandments. The term is generally construed to mean extramarital sexuality on the part of a married woman. Technically, Jewish legal authorities interpret adultery to mean intercourse between a married woman

and a man other than her husband. Nonetheless, nowadays—especially since the official ban on polygamy which
is now more than one thousand years old—rabbinical
opinion preponderantly opposes any extramarital relations between a married man and a woman who is not his
wife.

When it comes to premarital sexuality, a great deal more
debate has taken place, and Judaism in the current free-
wheeling ambience of the final years of the twentieth
century waffles. The rabbinic texts clearly state that sexual
relations should take place only between husband and
wife; that is probably why Jewish tradition and early
teaching urged young men and young women to marry
early, preferably in their late teens, for they recognized the
power of the sexual drive in young people. In talmudic
times it became a goal for a young man to be married off
by the time he was eighteen (and a young woman at even
an earlier age). If a man was not married by the time he
was twenty, the Talmud cautioned, God would curse him.

In the course of the last few centuries, things did
change. Young men wished to devote more and more
years to study so that they could reach ever higher on the
economic and professional ladder. A phenomenon known
as birth control came along and with each passing decade,
it seemed, new and more sophisticated methods evolved
where young people learned they could indulge in sexual
relations without marrying and without producing ba-
bies, and this certainly led to major changes in thought
and activities.

There is no verse in the Hebrew Bible or in the Mishna
or Talmud that specifically forbids premarital sex. The
aforementioned stern commentator of the 13th century,
Nahmanides, wrote on the subject: "Casual intercourse is
prohibited to the Jews only on authority of Rabbi Eliezer
ben Jacob's statement that except for such a ban, it might

happen that a brother might marry his sister, or a father his daughter. Of such a state the Torah speaks when it says "the earth will be filled with immorality."

Thus, this prohibition is seen as a somewhat convoluted way in which legal authorities sought textual justification for their rulings against premarital sex. It is only in Maimonides' classic *Mishneh Torah* in which is found a clear-cut Jewish religious legal ruling against sexual relations before marriage.

In our own time the distinguished president of Yeshiva University, Dr. Norman Lamm, commented on the subject as follows: "In the Jewish view it is insufficient to affirm that the act must have meaning; it must also have value. For Judaism the value in human sexuality comes only when the relationship involves two people who have committed themselves to one another and have made that commitment in a binding covenant recognized by God and society. The act of sexual union, the deepest personal statement that any human being can make, must be reserved for the moment of total oneness."

Inasmuch as more and more young Jewish men and women are not getting married until they are in their late twenties or thirties, modern Jewish thinkers on the subject seem to have relaxed their stringent views and they are far more permissive in this area than hitherto especially when the question involves a couple who sooner or later plan to tie the marital knot. This lenient attitude is based on the reality of the day, and of course applies far more to Conservative and Reform Jews than Orthodox Jews. In that latter community the strictures are still pretty severe.

In the closing years of the twentieth century a new issue has arisen among all Jews, one which has by no means found an easy solution: the question of male and female homosexuality. The Bible speaks quite clearly against homosexual acts (but avoids the question of homosexual inclinations). Such acts between men, Judaism declared, are an "abomination" and those who perform them should be punished by death. Modern Jewish thinkers, explaining the harshness of the biblical statement, cite the fact that the Bible sought to preserve the sanctity of the family and the obligation to rear children in a moral atmosphere, plus the Jewish contention that the world's moral depravity—then and now—had to be offset by a society that followed an ethical lifestyle.

Those in the Jewish community who take a far more liberal approach to homosexuals insist that these people were born that way and cannot help their disposition. The debate in various forms in the Jewish community goes on but virtually all segments of Judaism agree that homosexuals themselves should not be rejected by the Jewish community, even if one is utterly opposed to their lifestyle.

For reasons that remain unclear, lesbian women are regarded with far more compassion and tolerance than men. The debate on this overall issue is sure to continue for many years. It is probably the openness of modern society that has brought this previously hidden situation into the open.

CHAPTER SEVEN

Did Arranged Marriages of Past Work?

In Hebrew the word for a man is *eesh*; for a woman, *eesha*. In the word for man the Hebrew letter *yud* is added, while in the term for a woman there is another additional letter, *heh*. As any student of Hebrew knows, if you put those two letters together you form a name for God, *yah*. Thus, the talmudic sages explained, if the marriage is harmonious and happy, God's presence is almost palpable in that nuclear family. On the other hand, if there is disharmony and bickering, those letters do not come together to form God's name, but the original word for man and woman is akin to the word for fire, *esh*. Such a marriage is an unhappy union, consumed by fire.

The rabbis of old advised a new husband to "spend less than his means on food, up to his means on clothes, and beyond his means in honoring his wife and children." The rabbis of two millennia ago understood that when a marriage is arranged, and is then consummated, a great deal of tact, wisdom and effort must be exercised to keep both partners on an even keel, growing together emotionally and intellectually through the years. The wedding ceremony binding a man and a woman is a relatively short affair, but it is seen in Judaism as both a religious and legal contract, and it is stressed that both husband and wife must be afforded equal rights, and these rights must always be safeguarded.

There is a faint echo of weddings from the biblical days in our modern wedding ceremonies. Nonetheless there are subtle differences within individual Jewish communities, and even more drastic nuance changes during the course of the last centuries. Granted, the basic elements of the ceremony are the same but some customs adhered to in countries like India or the remote areas of the Moslem states in what used to be the Soviet Union are generic to those places. Many Jews from North Africa and certain Asian countries have adopted local traditions and incorporated them into the Jewish celebrations. The fear of the so-called "evil eye" often explains the origin of these customs, while other practices are designed to bring blessings on the new couple. The origins of some practices have been lost in time, but are usually still followed out of loyalty to one's parents or grandparents.

Essentially, when a wedding ceremony is planned and held, almost always followed by a lavish reception for family and friends, the hosts—knowingly or otherwise—bear in mind the brief biblical description of Laban, father of Leah and Rachel, getting set for his first daughter's wedding: "Laban gathered all the people of the place and made a feast." Later, when Jacob learned that he had been tricked into marrying the older sister, Leah, whom he did not love, and complains to his father-in-law, Laban replies: "Fulfill the (bridal) week of this one, and we will give you the other one also." Thus, we hear about a wedding reception, about a bridal week (the forerunner of our modern honeymoon), and about negotiations that often develop between in-laws, the groom, and occasionally, the bride.

Later the Bible talks of the strongman Samson, who has become a groom, and during the seven days that followed the wedding feast he challenged his companions with a riddle. He gave them the seven days of the festive period to come up with an answer. There are biblical and talmudic hints that the idea of a bridal procession originated in those far off days, as did the more or less discarded custom of a groom displaying his wife's virginity by holding up a blood-stained bedsheet.

Up until talmudic times, the wedding ceremony was divided into two parts: the first was *erusin* (sometimes called *kiddushin*), and generally translated as betrothal, and the second part was designated as *nisu'in*, which is the actual marriage. If the bride was virginal, a year ensued between the two events; if she was not, only a month separated the two rites. Today, the wedding ceremony with both elements takes place together under the wedding canopy. This coupling of the ceremonies dates from the Middle Ages when Jews began to sense that because of unsettled times it was wise not to have a whole year separate the young couple.

Of course, not all wedding ceremonies and receptions took place under happy and festive conditions. In the Ukraine, in the aftermath of the Bolshevik revolution when the Red and White armies battled each other for control of that vast region, the Jewish community was very large and always threatened by the Cossacks who delighted in killing defenseless Jews, between battles with the Bolsheviks. Many Ukrainian Jews decided that there was no future for them in that hapless place, and those who were married crossed the border into Poland, usually illegally, en route to new lives and homes in the United

States, South America and Palestine. But what of the 18-year-old Jewish girls? How could they join such migrations, without being married? In those unhappy years, 1917, 1918, 1919, thousands of young Jews were married hastily, sometimes two sisters one right after another, and the receptions were skipped. Once the young woman was formally, legally married to a Jewish young man, they could proceed to a new destination and a new life.

When the Nazi era began a few lucky German Jews had valid visas to enter Palestine and escape what was to happen in the decade ahead. Many of these visa-holders were young men, and they were called upon by rabbis, parents, friends to "marry"—to go through a fake wedding ceremony so that they could leave for Palestine with their "wives." That is how many hundreds of young Jewish women found haven in Palestine and escaped the Nazi inferno. Some of the couples decided to remain married, but most of them went through a quick "divorce," once they were in Palestine.

As was noted earlier, unlike today, most marriages were arranged in biblical, talmudic and post-talmudic times by parents; later the professional matchmaker, the *shadchan*, appeared on the scene. In ancient Israel, there was another way for young people to meet and in this instance the men and the women made their own choices.

Twice a year—on the fifteenth day of the Hebrew month *Av*, which falls during the summer, and on Yom Kippur, the Day of Atonement, which usually occurs in September or early October—all unmarried women who wished to meet an eligible bachelor and wed would don a white dress and step out of their native villages to nearby fields. There they would find the men, bachelors who wanted to get married, waiting eagerly. The women would try to look their best, and the men would circle them, looking, making small talk, trying to decide. The women of course looked back; probably the more aggressive among them called out to the men.

The system seemed to work for many years and was abandoned when the Romans conquered Israel and forced the Jews into exile. What was appealing about this method of picking a mate was that both the men and the women had equal rights to accept or reject a marriage offer. It sounds a bit like what probably happens in a singles resort.

*   *   *

In very early periods, when a couple became engaged the parents of both the prospective groom and bride held a formal ceremony, during which they put on paper a document known as *t'na'im*, Hebrew for conditions. The written agreement between both sides spelled out the time and date of the forthcoming marriage, as well as such matters as the financial obligations of both sides, including the dowry to be brought by the bride, and the amount of time that the bride's father undertook to support the couple while the new son-in-law pursued his studies. Today the ceremony of *t'na'im* is still observed in Orthodox (and some Conservative) families, as is the custom of a dowry.

There are, of course, poor young women who need financial help in order to get married. To this end many Jewish communities have developed a communal institution knows as *hachnasat kalah*, whose sole purpose is to make sure that no young woman be denied a chance to marry because she lacks the funds. In the early years of Israel's statehood, things were so tough that bridal gowns were practically an unobtainable luxury. One of America's most ardent supporters of the new state was the late Walter Lowdermilk, a world-renowned agricultural engineer who was sent by the United Nations to help Israel improve its agricultural productivity. His wife, when she learned about the shortage of bridal gowns, had a few of these garments sent in from the United States and spent the next few years altering gowns for the prospective brides in northern Israel. One estimate said she thus prepared hundreds of young women for their wedding day.

Among the minority of Jewish families that still observe the ceremony of *t'na'um* there is a custom that is seen only or at least primarily in Orthodox circles—after the document is completed, the parents smash a plate, and all those assembled shout *mazel tov!* (good luck!) This of course reminds those in attendance of the crushing of a glass by the groom under the wedding canopy at the very end of the wedding ceremony.

The dowry gift, known as a *mohar* and practiced more among Sephardic families than Ashkenazim, nowadays is actually not entirely dispensed with—it is customary for the parents of both the bride and groom to give extensive gifts to the young couple, and without saying so, everyone understands that the gifts take care of the ancient *mohar* tradition.

In Israel, there are already a number of individual customs focused on marriage. When a baby boy is born, a cedar tree is planted, and for a baby girl a cypress is rooted. The planting is done on *Tu B'Shvat*, Jewish Arbor Day. When they grow up, it is traditional to cut branches from these trees and use them in holding aloft the wedding canopy.

Another Israeli practice is provision of housing. Because buying an apartment is a high economic priority, parents, as soon as a child is born, begin to save so that they can give their child—as a wedding present—a ready-to-use place to live.

Many of the wedding gifts provided by parents in the United States take the form of furniture, dishes, silverware, with each set of parents deciding between the two of them who gives what. One gift that traditionally is given to the groom by the prospective father-in-law is the *tallit*, the prayer shawl that is used at worship services. This usually follows after the young man has given his future wife a diamond engagement ring.

Probably all Orthodox brides-to-be and a great many Conservative brides-to-be visit the *mikvah*, the ritual bath in the week prior to the wedding. (In Israel this is required by law; the rabbi officiating at the wedding will not proceed unless he sees a valid certificate attesting to the fact that the young lady adhered to this injunction.) On the occasion of her visit to a *mikvah* before the wedding, the bride is allowed to bring along a woman companion. Otherwise, during married life, after her menstrual cycle she normally proceeds there on her own, out of a sense of modesty.

The question of not seeing each other prior to the wedding is a local custom for most brides and grooms. Mostly, in the United States, the young couple abstains from seeing each other on the day of the wedding; in some Asian and North African countries, they refrain from visiting one another for a whole week. In western countries, a bride and a groom, together or separately, if their parents are deceased, may visit the graves of their mothers and fathers. Some will explain that they wish to share their happiness with their departed parents, while others may state that they wish their parents will pray for them, that the marriage will be a happy and successful one.

As the couple prepares for the day of their wedding, they sense that they are being transformed into new people, and that all of their previous sins, if any, have been forgiven.

CHAPTER EIGHT

God Said: "It Is Not Good for Man to Be Alone"

The Bible states very clearly and directly, "Two are better than one." And in the opening pages of Genesis, God declares: "It is not good for man to be alone, I will make a fitting helper for him."

In the closing years of the twentieth century, when life for virtually everyone is lived at a super-frenetic pace, a person who does not have a lifetime companion—a husband or wife—is missing out on one of life's most natural, gratifying dimensions. A spouse is someone with whom to enjoy the everyday pleasures or problems and heartaches; a spouse can bolster the other partner in the marriage in times of need or crisis, and in so doing, over the course of time, a bond between them grows ever-stronger, and life as a whole does not loom quite so daunting.

A long-time ago Proverbs announced that "a virtuous woman is a crown to her husband." The same biblical volume, a little later, adds: "A home and riches are the inheritance of fathers, but a prudent wife is from the Lord." The Bible placed such strong emphasis on a good marriage that a groom was instructed in Deuteronomy: "When a man has taken a bride, he shall not go out with the army or be assigned to it for any purpose. He shall be exempt one year for the sake of his household, to give happiness to the woman he has married." Imagine, a year-long honeymoon!

In the Apocrypha, those volumes that were left out of the canon of the Bible, Ben Sira declares: "Happy is the man who has a good wife, the number of his days will be doubled. A noble wife gladdens her husband, and he lives out his years in peace. A good wife is good fortune."

Despite all the ancient tales that have come down to us, that King David was a great womanizer, and that King Solomon had a "thousand" wives, the fact is in biblical times and talmudic times, almost all the rabbis and sages had one wife and practiced monogamy, even though at the time polygamy was permissible. The more than two thousand rabbis whose opinions, commentaries and inter-pretations form the works of the Talmud give a great deal of time and thought to finding the most successful paths to a happy marriage. Although they were not schooled in modern psychology, reading and studying them today inevitably results in a profound sense of admiration for their views. It is as though they lived here and now, with us, and understood the weaknesses and problems of modern men and women.

These are some of the talmudic observations: "Any man who has no wife is not a man, i.e., a complete human being, for it is written (in Genesis): 'Male and female He created them, and blessed them, and He called *their* name man.'…. If the wife you have is small, bend to her and whisper all.… A man's home is his wife."

In our own day, some of the comments about wives and

husbands have evolved from hard lives in the east European *shtetl* of old, and from the lives of early immigrants to the western world. Some of these observations may seem cynical, but they are meant to convey a hard lesson. For example, Yiddish writers a century ago used to say: "Old maids make devoted wives.... The man who is too good for the world is no good to his wife,"... "An unmarried woman should preen herself for the young men she may meet; a wife should be pretty for her husband."... "When the wife is fat, she bakes round loaves."... "Sometimes even a shrewish wife can be right."... "A wife is a bit of a dove and a bit of a devil."... "A wife can make the man the master or the slave."

Even in far-off talmudic days, certain situations existed that sound very familiar today, indeed, as if they were in yesterday's newspaper. The Talmud advised: "A henpecked husband can't get relief in court.... A faithless husband makes a faithless wife.... It is better for a woman that she have one useless husband than ten wealthy children."

One of the medieval customs that has come down to us is the ethical will, in which a parent—generally a father—instructs his son (or his daughter) on how to live a good life. These wills included all kinds of advice, not the least of which were comments on marital life. Asher ben Yechiel, who lived in the thirteenth century, wrote in his will: "Never be angry with your wife. If you put her from you with your left hand, do not delay in drawing her to you with your right hand." Joseph ibn Caspi, in the same time period, wrote: "Marry a wife of good family, beautiful in form and character. Pay no heed to money, for true wealth consists of enough bread to eat and clothes to wear."... In the fourteenth century, Eleazar of Mayence wrote: "My daughters must respect their husbands exceedingly, and must be invariably amiable to them. Husbands, on their part, must honor their wives more than themselves, and treat them with tender consideration."

The fourteenth century religious philosopher Israel ibn al-Nakawa took a very practical attitude toward married life. He said:

> If a man is so fortunate as to have found a good wife, he shall never miss anything. Though he may be poor, he may regard himself as rich. As the Bible intimates (in the book of Proverbs), it is easier to obtain precious stones than to find a good wife. Where there is love and trust between husband and wife, there will be riches and contentment; but if they hate each other, the contrary must happen. They shall miss everything if their hearts are divided. A good wife sets a crown upon the head of her husband; a bad one is a canker to his bones. A good wife is one who manages his affairs correctly, watches his money, assists him with all her might, gives him good advice, and does not press him to spend more than is necessary. She supervises the needs of the home and the education of the children, and does so diligently. Moreover, she tries to please her husband, and is always eager to cheer and comfort him, and to free him from worry. She tries to understand his needs and to study his moods, and takes delight in serving him, because she loves him deeply. Besides, she treats her husband's family fairly, not playing the snob towards them if she herself happens to belong to a higher station.
>
> Marriage is not a one-sided affair. The man has obligations, no less than the woman. First, he must have as high a regard for his wife as for his own self, and honor her accordingly. She brings him completion and blessing, and it is his duty to realize it. He must be particularly careful to provide the needs of the home, for lack of provision is often the beginning of strife. Let a man sacrifice his personal wants, in order to provide the more abundantly for his wife and children. Above all, let him

treat his wife with love and sympathy, seeing she is part of him, and depends on him, as he depends upon God. He must never treat her violently, nor abuse her, nor deceive her. Where a man shows deference to his wife, and creates an atmosphere of love and harmony, there the Divine spirit finds satisfaction.

A man shouldtry to marry a woman of a good family, enjoying an honorable and unblemished reputation. He must not think of the woman's beauty but of the quality of her acts. A woman's supreme beauty is not in her face but in her fair and just deeds. That is why wise men have repeatedly warned against marrying a woman for her beauty. Many a wealthy house has been ruined by folly, while a good and intelligent woman, though poor, enriches a house.

A man ought to go to any length in order to marry a properly qualified woman, especially the daughter of a learned man. But if a man married for money, misery is sure to ensue. The children of such a marriage are likely to be of inferior quality. Similar results are in store for other kinds of unsuitable unions.

Faithfulness to each other is one of the essential conditions of the marriage. If a man engages in adultery, it is as if he became an idolater. The same is true of a woman. People who practice adultery, the rabbis taught, are regarded as breakers of the Ten Commandments, for, once entered upon that course, there is no sin they are not likely to commit as a sequel, if circumstances demand it. One of the merits of a suitable marriage and an early one is that it prevents the formation of lewd habits and perverse practices.

Marriage has come a long way since ancient times. Among the Jews in ancient Judea (Palestine) the father of a young, unmarried woman was looked upon as her owner. And when she married, this ownership was transferred to her husband. The Hebrew word for a husband, *ba'al*, still in use today, literally means a master. Thus a *ba'al bayit* is the master of the house, while the wife—also still in use today in Israel—is called *eesha*, which literally means woman. Thus a husband was the master, and the wife was his woman. At times the word master was turned into a verb, and was used to mean the husband mastered her, or married her.

As late as the seventeenth century, Jewish young women were taught by mothers to be compliant and diffident, and obedient, vis-a-vis their husbands. One young woman about to get married was handed a ten-point letter by her mother, instructing her to follow these "commandments" in order to have a happy marriage. Summarized and paraphrased from an ethical work titled *Lev Tov*, the mother wrote to her daughter: 1. Be aware of your husband's anger; when he is cross, don't be jolly, and when he is jolly, you don't be cross. 2. Find out about his preferences in eating, try to have his meals ready on time, for hunger does not do anyone any good. 3. When he is asleep, guard his sleep that he should not be wakened; if he does not get a good night's sleep, he may become angry. 4. Be thrifty, be careful with your husband's money. 5. Don't try to learn his secrets. If you do, do not tell them to anyone in the world. 6. Learn who your husband likes or dislikes. Don't like his enemies, and don't dislike his friends. 7. Don't be contrary with him. Do everything he tells you. 8. Don't expect anything of him that he may think is difficult. If you do, he may take a dislike to you. 9. Heed the requests he may make of you, and wait in turn for him to love you for it. Then he will be your slave, serve you with joy and love you. 10. Guard against jealousy. Don't make him jealous in any way. Don't say anything that may upset or hurt him. Let him have his way in everything.

Even in the most traditional families, it is doubtful that

a woman in this day and age would give her daughter such instructions.

*   *   *

Throughout the ages, from biblical times down to our own, a wedding was always a special occasion where rejoicing abounded. Until recent years, the wedding ceremony signified the bride's voluntary entry into the home of the groom. Indeed, the *chupah*—the wedding canopy—is interpreted as being the groom's symbolic home, and when the bride enters it she is making a statement: she is prepared to enter her future husband's home and live there with him.

In the United States, and in most western countries, the wedding ceremony and the reception that follows are generally lavish, joyous occasions. There are also, no doubt, wedding ceremonies held at a rabbi's study, with a very modest meal for a small number of people—it all depends on the circumstances. In the North African, Asian and some Moslem-dominated countries in the former Soviet Union, the wedding ceremony in the synagogue was often followed by a week-long series of festive celebrations.

Guests invited to a modern Jewish wedding in the United States often number between two hundred and three hundred, and include relatives far and wide, friends, neighbors and colleagues at work. Non-Jews who are invited generally have a great time, for often it is the first time they are exposed to a healthy dose of Jewish music, food, dancing, and of course the religious marriage ceremony. In fact, one of the Jewish wedding's quaint customs is for the bride and groom to be raised on chairs, while the music plays, and for everyone present to clap along. Sometimes, some of the parents are also lifted on chairs.

Word has gotten out that at some recent non-Jewish affairs, the bride and groom have also been elevated in a burst of joy. Ecumenism at work!

One peculiarity about weddings in Israel involves the invited guests. Because the country is largely informal, wedding receptions naturally follow suit. Yes, there are formal weddings at deluxe hotels, and sometimes the guests are advised to come in black tie. And of course on an agricultural *kibbutz*, everyone comes dressed in jeans, open shirts, sandals, and the men can't wait to remove the skull caps they have donned while the rabbi recites the requisite blessings.

In Israel's urban centers, most families hosting a wedding for their children invite everyone—including relatives, friends, neighbors, the mailman, the trash collectors, the policeman on the beat, and the couple's teachers when they were small children. Some dress up, some come in shorts, some bring presents to the wedding, but all have a very jolly time!

CHAPTER NINE

In Judaism, Married Sexual Life Is Just Fine

The Jewish people, Judaism teaches, must strive always to become a holy people. By being a holy people, Jews are instructed, you become an exemplary people, a model for all people to emulate. Jews historically have never felt quite comfortable with the designation of "the chosen people," but being a holy people, which everyone can emulate, that's quite different. The term "a chosen people" implies that Jews are inherently better, superior than other peoples—something that Jews are the first to shrug off. Whenever a Jew is arrested for a minor or major crime, many Jews turn to each other and, in effect, say, verbally or silently, "See, I told you, we're just like everyone else." The comment is generally followed by an inner sigh of disappointment, for if we were really a holy people—as the Bible says God wants us to be—then we wouldn't have any criminals among us. And that is why it is doubly painful to hear about a criminal in the Jewish community who is ostensibly religious. From him, especially, we expected better!

Jewish marriage from ancient times to today continues to emphasize holiness, particularly when two strangers come together and fashion a new life. Traditional Judaism has never ceased to encourage *taharat hamishpachah*—family purity. In Judaism marital fidelity is *sine qua non*; family purity goes far beyond that basic precept.

In the Bible, in the book of Leviticus, Jews are warned about having sexual intercourse with a woman when she has her monthly menstrual flow. "Do not come near a woman in her period of uncleanness," the Bibles states clearly. The talmudic rabbis ordered that a man shall not "go near" a menstruating woman for a full fourteen days, to encompass the time of her flow and a full week afterwards before marital relations can be resumed. And then they added that before relations are resumed, she should purify herself ritually in a *mikvah*.

There are some rabbis who maintain that this enforced separation between husband and wife each month actually bolsters their sexual life together; they see it as a kind of monthly renewal. There are also some—by no means all—feminists who insist that this whole ancient Jewish practice should be abandoned for it is really a form of misogyny. They stress modern scientific findings that declare that relations during the menstrual cycle are perfectly acceptable and natural.

The Orthodox community by and large observes this ancient regulation of family purity, while among Reform Jews the practice has been all but abandoned. Among Conservative Jews there are mixed signals: a number of rabbis encourage observance of this ruling, while among others the practice has been expanded, i.e., the husband

and wife go to the *mikvah* together (there are separate facilities for them) on a monthly basis.

*   *   *

Judaism traditionally has regarded married sexual life as a necessary social institution which assures the continuity of the Jewish family, and hence the Jewish people. The rabbis and sages, all through the centuries, have come to look on marriage as a source of positive joys—parental joy, and the joy of union between a husband and his wife. Indeed, Judaism saw—and continues to this day to see— marriage as *kiddushin*: sanctification. Thus, the wedding ceremony and the subsequent married life of the new couple are viewed as holy events, elevating the recently married couple to a new status in life—that of a sanctified pair, united with vast numbers of other sanctified couples, all of them aimed at attaining new plateaus of secular sacredness and piety.

Some two and a half thousand years ago, following the destruction of the Holy Temple in Jerusalem, when the Jews had been carried off to exile and captivity in Babylonia, the rabbis of that time and place taught that even sensual passion, known as the *yetser ha'ra*, or the evil inclination, had its good side. Because, it was explained, without it no one would build a house, no one would take a wife, and no one would beget children.

Perhaps the fact that the Hebrew Bible does not have a word for marriage is not so peculiar, for marriage in those ancient days was looked upon as a communion, a covenant between husband and wife, or more precisely "a sanctification." As is known, there are no celibate monks or nuns in Judaism; even the famous monastic Essenes who lived near the Dead Sea are said by some scholars to have had wives. Several thousand years ago the rabbis taught that a "Jew who has no wife lives without joy, without blessing, without goodness." They also stated that a "Jew who has no wife is not a man." This ancient rabbinical determination that Jews should all marry and raise families was so strong that up to the third century a man and a woman could wed merely by expressing mutual consent followed by consummation. There was no need to live together for any length of time as Roman or Anglo-Saxon law required. Although the law was changed in the third century, people still practiced it. To protect the children that might be born as the result of such unions, it was decreed that they would have virtually the same legal rights as children whose parents had undergone a traditional wedding ceremony.

Despite the rabbis' liberal rulings in marital matters, they were quite stringent in certain other matters. For example, no obscene talk was to be done by the married couple (it was actually grounds for divorce); intercourse with a pregnant wife was proscribed, although the rabbis realized it was a difficult regulation to enforce.

*　*　*

Surprisingly, in this day and age, the most popular day of the week to get married—during the Middle Ages— was Friday. It was seen by most Jews of the time as a convenient day, coming at the end of the work week, and if there were no plans for a formal honeymoon, as often there were not (purely for financial reasons) at least the young couple had the Sabbath to look forward to.

Other popular days of the week that were chosen for a wedding included Tuesday: it was considered a "lucky" day because on the third day of the week of creation, as told in Genesis, God looked around at His handiwork and said twice, This is good (on other days He only said it once); Wednesday: was a day frequently chosen by virginal brides; Thursday: was traditionally selected for a wedding by a widow who was remarrying.

Saturdays and holidays were never chosen for weddings. In the Middle Ages, some of the customs that have since been abandoned included ashes strewn on the bridal couple's heads to remind them of the solemnity of the wedding ceremony. In some German communities the bride and groom wore mourning clothes, at least partially, as a reminder that even in their most joyous of occasions, they should remember the destruction of the Holy Temple in Jerusalem.

Practically all modern Jewish weddings include the groom's stomping and breaking a glass at the end of the actual ceremony, as a reminder of the Temple's destruction. At some weddings unmarried young women vie for a fragmented shard from the broken glass; it seems to be a good luck omen for some, reminding us, of course, of the bride's tossing of her bouquet to a group of unmarried women friends. This practice, by the way, began as a tradition at Christian weddings, but in recent years some Reform Jewish weddings have adopted it.

Essentially, all Jewish weddings all over the world are the same, with some distinct customs having been incorporated from the local culture where the bridal couple was raised. Thus, the Asian-North African henna smearing on the fingernails and the palms of the hand by the bride and her women guests, a custom that the Eastern Jews now living in Israel have maintained. The Hasidic weddings, both in pre-World War II Europe and today in the United States and other western countries, include frenzied male dancing, in which an open bottle of vodka is often balanced on the head—in imitation, of all people—of the anti-Semitic Cossacks of Russia. In the United States, of course, depending on the religiosity and traditions of the families hosting the wedding, dancing can range from Israeli horas, men-only Hasidic group numbers, women only line dancing, all the way to the most heated rock and roll performances.

As stated, the wedding ceremony itself is essentially direct and straightforward. There is a processional in which the bride's parents escort her down the aisle and symbolically hand her over to the groom, who then brings her to the *chupah*, symbolically the couple's new home, formerly his alone, which will now become their place of residence. Everything else at the wedding is tacked on for the sake of creating an atmosphere of joy, in a suitable religious and legal setting, with the legal document that the groom hands the bride (the *ketubah*) indicating the legality of the transaction, and the wedding rings that both the bride and groom wear attesting to their new status as a married pair.

Some of the Middle Ages wedding customs that have not come down to our time may very well hark back to biblical days but we have no concrete proof. For example, the bride and groom—standing under the wedding canopy—wore crowns fashioned from roses and myrtles, and sometimes olive branches, intertwined amid crimson and golden threads. The closest a Jewish wedding still comes to this is a *kibbutz* wedding in Israel, where the couple, living all their lives in an agricultural village, decorate their heads with floral crowns. There is a passage in the book of Isaiah that speaks of a groom who decorates himself "with a garland and a bride adorns herself with jewels." Perhaps this is where this ancient tradition arose.

In ancient Persia, now Iran, the bride and groom had to stride over thrown nuts and wheat scattered in the aisle; a few days before the wedding barley seeds were planted in a vase that was emptied at the wedding and cast over the couple's head, symbolizing fertility. At some Eastern weddings a live fish was kept in a bowl and deliberately placed in the path of the bridal couple. Before they were allowed to proceed they had to jump over the fish bowl three times, and this too symbolized the hope for fertility.

Some wedding receptions continued for seven days, and usually included singers and jesters whose job it was to make the bridal couple and their guests merry throughout the festive period. In some cases the festivities continued right into the Sabbath day, when Jewish musicians and entertainers stepped aside and were replaced for the day by non-Jewish performers.

A special feature of Jewish weddings, beginning in the seventeenth century, and carried out in Ashkenazic and Sephardic celebrations, was the carefully staged jesting play, in which the jester would sing for all to hear caustic material aimed at everyone—the bridal couple's parents, the bridal couple, the siblings, the rabbi. It was a kind of wedding-wide roast which everyone knew was proffered in good fun. It was generally offered while the guests were sitting down to their meal after the actual wedding ceremony, when everyone was in a mirthful, joyful mood. Often the local rabbi joined in the fun. The same rabbi who married the pair under the *chupah*, in a somber, happy, traditional ceremony, would be invited to say a few words after the meal and this often became his opportunity to display his wit and humor. The whole humor-roast part of the wedding was often linked to the gifts that guests had brought. It was not unusual for a professional jester to look into the presents brought to the table by a relative, and to comment on them entertainingly, while everyone laughed—until their own gifts were held up for public scrutiny.

*   *   *

The *ketubah*, the Jewish marriage contract, is a post-biblical institution. Its chief purpose seems to have been for a woman to be able to show the world that if she is alone, it is because her former husband had divorced her by giving her this document. It is also a legal document between a groom and his bride in which he promises to provide for her, both in the time when they are married and live as man and wife, and also—if he dies or if he divorces her—subsequently.

The document itself is written in Aramaic, the lingua franca of olden times in the Middle East. Centuries ago, especially in Eastern communities, it was embellished by artists who often custom-made each one to fit a particular couple. For example, if the husband in one case was a successful butcher, the *ketubah* might include artistic touches indicating the kind of work he did. The artistic, quite beautiful, *ketubah* documents came on bad times a few centuries ago, when many people began using simple, printed forms. However, the artistic *ketubah* has been rediscovered and there are now many artists who specialize in doing them.

Once again, they are customizing them to the husband's vocation. However, nowadays, when the young wife is more than likely to be an educated woman with a professional degree or two, along with her husband, the *ketubah* of this era is often bedecked with symbols for both of them. One recent example displayed two physicians, one male and the other female, stethoscopes hanging from their necks, checking out some X-rays. Sure enough, the young couple were both practicing radiologists. Another recent custom involving the artistic *ketubah* is the married couple celebrating a silver or golden wedding anniversary. Older and possibly retired, they have become the recipients of a specially prepared *ketubah* that highlights their earlier marriage and their current status in life.

Most historians agree that the original *ketubah* dates from the time of the Babylonian exile which followed the destruction of the Holy Temple in the year 586 BCE. The Jews had been exiled, in many cases without their families, and in the course of time many of the men had married local women.

When they were allowed to return home, the scribes and leaders Ezra and Nehemiah insisted—in an attempt to maintain the purity and continuity of the Jewish people—that the men divorce their foreign wives and marry Jewish women. The *ketubah* sprang into existence to ensure that the Jewish husbands understood the responsibility they were undertaking, and also to protect the Jewish wives.

It was a somewhat harsh way to restore the Jewish family and to ascertain that the pagan women not influence the Jewish men with whom they had been living. Apparently it worked, and the Jewishness of the emerging families was upheld.

*   *   *

Young Jews about to embark on the voyage of their lives, the voyage known as marriage, by and large harbor misinformation about Judaism's attitude towards the sexual side of marital bliss. Many mistakenly believe that Judaism has nothing to say about sex in marriage, or if it does it's generally an admonition of one kind or another. Nothing could be further from the truth!

Many rabbis have noted that young couples who visit them before the wedding suddenly seem to become tongue-tied when sexual matters come up. They act embarrassed, as though it is bad manners to discuss this with a rabbi—and the rabbi would like nothing more than to assure them that Judaism sees sexual bliss in marriage as a *mitzvah*, as a commandment.

Simply stated, Judaism believes that marriage is an ideal lifestyle, and sex in marriage is a God-given gift, to be enjoyed and appreciated—both for the obvious goal of procreation and for the intimate companionship to which it leads. After all, doesn't the biblical phrase, "it is not good for man to be alone," mean that getting married is an objective for all people to desire?

To demonstrate how important marriage is regarded in Judaism, the talmudic rabbis taught that in order to finance a wedding, a poor orphan who owned a holy Scroll of the Torah was permitted to sell it—and such a sale was not permitted for any other reason. In Temple days, the High Priests were required to be married. And if a funeral procession and a wedding party approached a street intersection simultaneously, the wedding procession took precedence.

The ancient rabbis taught that they valued a single person, not only a married person. They felt compassion for a widowed person, or one who was divorced, or one who had simply never been married. But, they stressed, the ideal situation was a married couple, who shared their life and built a family.

Judaism long ago recognized that human beings are both spiritual and sexual by nature, and both sides should be nurtured. One of the great commentators, Nachmanides, went so far as to say that when a "husband is in union with his wife, the *shechinah*, the divine presence, is with them."

The Jewish view of a woman's sexual needs and pleasures was quite obviously centuries ahead of its time. Not only does Jewish tradition and Jewish law stipulate that in every marriage a wife is entitled to receive from her husband an adequate provision of food and clothes and shelter but also satisfaction of her conjugal rights. What's more, a wife in Judaism is to be courted with sensitivity; for example, since the eve of the Sabbath, i.e., Friday evening, ushered in a day of rest and tranquility, and was often recommended as a propitious time for sexual union, the husband was advised to approach his wife by reciting to her selections from the biblical volume, the *Song of Songs*—a love-smitten ode to love and to women in general.

Judaism emphasized that a husband should not force himself on his wife, and he should not approach her while in a state of drunkenness, and any man who sought only his own sexual satisfaction was described as a "thief who steals away in the night."

The Jewish religion is described as a religion of ideals and deeds. Thus, Judaism teaches, if a married man—a happily married man—finds himself casting lustful glances at a beautiful woman other than his wife, he is advised not to be overly concerned. His looking and even his thinking are only fantasies; were he to act them out, that would be entirely different. Infidelity is a sinful act and is seen as a transgression not only against a spouse but also against God.

CHAPTER TEN

Changing Customs: The Groom Wore an Engagement Ring

Oddly, the engagement ring that brides-to-be proudly flash around was worn by the groom-to-be in Jewish communities during the Middle Ages. And even more oddly, the ring was presented to him by his future father-in-law. Nevertheless, on the morning of the wedding day, the bride received a golden engagement ring from her future husband. In fact, at one point, in the Italian Jewish community, the rabbis felt obligated to issue an edict stating that a man might not wear more than one ring and that it could be put on any finger, of either hand, while a woman was permitted to wear two rings, or at the most three. This *ukase* was issued because the rabbis of the time felt that men and women were displaying far too many rings, ostentatiously, and this could lead to inter-communal jealousies.

There was during this period another kind of wedding ring—the betrothal ring, which may be seen today in various museums. It was not meant to be worn normally, but only to be worn briefly during the wedding rite. Most of these ornamental bands portrayed, in gold, silver or some other precious metal, the synagogue, and sometimes a version of the Holy Temple that once stood in Jerusalem. Often the term *mazal tov* was inscribed into the ring, and sometimes a sprig of myrtle was inserted into it. A ring similar in design dating back to the fourth century C.E. was discovered in a Roman tomb, indicating that betrothal loops may well have been in use long before the Middle Ages. Presumably, after the wedding ceremony the ornate betrothal ring was returned to the officiating rabbi to be used in another forthcoming ceremony.

The rings that the bride and groom wore were totally different. These were simple gold bands, and in reality symbolized the gift of money that in ancient times a groom gave before he could marry his bride. The simple gold bands worn today by all married couples reflects this ancient tradition. Interestingly, by the ninth century Pope Nicholas introduced the gold wedding band to Christian wedding ceremonies.

*   *   *

In her charming book on *shtetl* life, Miriam Shomer Zunser captured the spirit of the very special kind of dancing that takes place at traditional Jewish wedding receptions. She writes: "About this dancing at a Jewish wedding: there is nothing at all that I can compare with it to convey its spirit. You dance not because you know how, but because the spirit moves you. Outside of the prohibition of men dancing with women there are no restrictions, or prearranged or practiced steps or forms. Women may dance with women and men with men if they so choose, but that too is not necessary. There is no order about the dance. Each person, as the impulse moves him, gets up and dances. Old and young, great and small, dance separately, or opposite each other. When the fiddles strike up a merry strain, and the cornet blows, when the drums boom and the tambourines jingle, they stamp their feet, clap their hands, lift their skirts and make steps—any kind of steps! If you are a man you lift your coattails and hop around. If you are a woman you grab a neighbor, whirl about with her, or go backward and forward in front of her, improvising as you dance. A group of people will form a ring and dance in a circle, each one creating his own steps, just so long as he keeps time with the music. If you are somebody of any importance at the wedding, the dancing ring will probably form around you. Dancing at a Jewish wedding (not a modern American one, of course) means a bodily expression of joy. And, indeed, if one cannot or will not move one's body or feet, one can certainly carry on with one's hands. Waving arms and snapping fingers were very acceptable substitutes for dancing."

This was how the *shtetl* wedding—two hundred years ago, in eastern Europe—was celebrated. Today's modern American Jewish weddings, a half-century after the Zunser book was published, is quite different from that of the *shtetl*. Nevertheless, more and more Jewish weddings have begun to bring back traditional Jewish dance music—the popular Israeli hora is in, as is klezmer music, as well as other Jewish dance music. It depends on what the hosts tell the band they want, which is usually based on how traditional and knowledgeable the wedding guests are.

One of the most beautiful, moving and charming features of a traditional Jewish wedding is the "mezenek dance." It is a special performance in which virtually the entire group of guests, including the bride and groom, form a vast line, everyone holding hands or letting go for a moment so they can join in the rhythmic clapping. The dance is dedicated to the marriage of the youngest child of that particular set of parents, indicating that God has blessed them and they have lived to attend their "baby's" wedding date.

Anyone who has ever attended a few Jewish wedding receptions is more than likely to recognize the special melody that is reserved for this feature of the wedding. What happens, almost instantly when the particular music begins, is for chairs to start moving, and the parents are propelled to a pair of seats in the middle of the floor. A circle quickly forms, hands clapping and swaying and singing ensue, and the parents, now seated in the midst of their friends and family, are all smiles. It's a memorable feature of the wedding, sure not to be forgotten.

It doesn't however always go smoothly, especially when the youngest child does marry, but his older sibling just got divorced, or if an older sister has reached her late thirties and has never married. In those circumstances, each family must decide for itself whether they want to enjoy the "mezenek dance" or skip it, perhaps for another time.

One thing is sure: the special tune set aside only for this feature of the wedding is very catchy, happy, memorable, and should be enjoyed by all, especially the parents, if circumstances warrant.

One of the most popular *shtetl* dance forms that has been included in many western Jewish weddings is the handkerchief dance. The bride is raised on a chair and the groom on another (this is at the reception, following the wedding ceremony). Each holds the corner of a decorative handkerchief between the two of them while a circle of dancers below whirl them around rhythmically. Sometimes the bride and groom dance slowly on the dance floor with a handkerchief between them. Guests surround them and cheer them on; sometimes this same dance routine is followed by either or both sets of parents, and even by grandparents.

* * *

In Poland, beginning in the fifteenth century, communal leaders felt obligated to issue ordinances limiting the amount of money that could be spent for a wedding. The rationale was quite logical: some parents, in their desire to arrange a splendid wedding, went to extremes and bankrupted themselves. In the course of time, it was felt that these people would apply to the communal funds for maintenance, and this of course would reduce the communal treasury. It was also felt that a very sumptuous wedding, with fancy clothes and over-generous food at the reception, would in all likelihood lead to negative attitudes on the part of non-Jewish neighbors and colleagues. Some of the restrictions listed the foods that could be served and the clothes that could be worn.

There were other restrictions in both Poland and Germany. One ruling stated that Jewish domestic workers and other employees could not marry unless the community as a whole voted by at least two-thirds to approve such a marriage. Another ordinance in those days did not permit a groom to settle in the hometown of his bride unless he brought with him a minimum sum of money.

For many years there was little opportunity for Ashkenazic and Sephardic Jews to meet, get to know each other and marry. A Sephardic man who wished to marry an Ashkenazic woman was regarded somewhat grudgingly as acceptable, it being expected however that the wife would learn Sephardic mores and adopt them. The Sephardic leaders of the time looked with askance on

Sephardic women who wished to marry Ashkenazic men, and tried to block such unions, usually unsuccessfully.

Over a period of centuries this attitude on the part of the Sephardic leaders was relaxed, and most of them accepted inter-marriages between the two groups. However, even to this day, both in the United States and Israel, Sephardic leaders—and parents—seem to have an inherent preference for their children to wed Sephardic spouses.

* * *

In some families, where a parent is deceased and not able to take part in a child's wedding, it is customary for the officiating rabbi to recite a special prayer at the wedding ceremony in honor of that parent.

Nowadays, when so many young people, Jews included, get married, then divorce and remarry, the second marriage sometimes is played down—i.e., there is a brief ceremony in the rabbi's study with parents and siblings—and sometimes children of the couple—in attendance. And sometimes the second marriage is a full-fledged wedding, *chupah* and all. If the parents of the bride and groom are living, they join the bridal couple under the canopy, as do, often, children of the couple's previous marriages. Occasionally it looks like a crowd scene!

In 1942 the great Jewish community of Spain was told either to convert to Catholicism or face expulsion from the country. Fearful, many Jews converted; large numbers of other Jews chose to leave, and began inter alia to settle in the western hemisphere that Columbus had discovered. Still others opted to live a double life: secretly observing Jewish rituals and customs, but claiming to be Catholics. History has dubbed them Marranos, although today they prefer to be called Conversos.

Weddings for them became problematic. According to Cecil Roth, the eminent historian, what they frequently did was appear in church—bride and groom—and undergo a Catholic wedding ceremony. They would then hurry back home, retreat to their secret rooms, and in the presence of trusted friends and family marry again, only this time in a Jewish ceremony. Sometimes they had to postpone the Jewish wedding ceremony until they left Spain (and later Portugal) and established themselves as Jews in their new homes. This special remarriage rite came to be known among Jewish communities in the western hemisphere, and in England and Holland where many settled, as being especially needed by couples "come from Portugal."

CHAPTER ELEVEN

Dancing Before the Bride Is A *Mitzvah!*

In the United States today, and most probably in all western countries, the only special attention paid to the reception meal after the wedding ceremony is that it be kosher (in most cases), lavish, sumptuous and befitting a wedding. To digress for a moment: Obviously kosher meals are de rigueur at Orthodox and many Conservative families' wedding celebrations. Since Reform Judaism pays no heed to kosher food laws, these are of no consequence to Reform families. But since kosher food does cost more than non-kosher food, wedding hosts sometimes skimp and provide a frozen, kosher meal only to those guests known to observe these laws.

It appears to be a somewhat unseemly way to arrange a Jewish *simcha*—a joyous occasion—but this is the way things are in the final years of the twentieth century.

At traditional Moroccan Jewish weddings, the menu always includes fish, a symbol of fertility. Music—happy, rhythmic music—is regarded as a principal requisite at all

Jewish weddings. The Bible and the Apocrypha mention timbrels and other musical instruments. For many years it was customary for a solo flutist to play before the bride and groom, but for some unknown reason this is no longer done. Since it is considered a *mitzvah*—a religious commandment, or a good deed—"to gladden the groom and bride," with choral and instrumental numbers, rabbis often led wedding guests in greeting the bridal pair in both religious and non-traditional songs. The biblical tome, *Song of Songs*, a very love-smitten work, lists "dancing with two swords," interpreted by some to mean a bride's dancing with elation while defending herself against any suitors but her husband.

A talmudic question reads: "How should one dance before the bride?" The response is given of scholars who danced before the bride as an act of religious devotion. One ancient rabbi, Judah bar Ilai, would sing and dance before a bride while clutching a myrtle twig, a symbol of good luck. Another rabbi cited in the Talmud, Samuel bar Rav Isaac, continued to sing and dance before new brides, even when he was quite old, all the time grasping a myrtle branch. When he died, the eulogies stressed that he had been a great man, notably because he had brought so much joy to numerous wedding celebrations.

By the sixteenth century, dancing modes had changed: men at a wedding reception would form a circle and dance with the groom, while women would encircle the bride and cavort with her. The custom began in Venice, at the time a large and prosperous Jewish community. Eventually the group dance—now designated as a *mitzvah* dance—spread to most other communities in Europe and North Africa. However, in the nineteenth century, the prevalent wedding dance style was for men to dance with the bride, provided each held opposite corners of a handkerchief between them. In the east European *shtetl* it was traditional for the hired jester—the *badchan*—to summon the dancers to step onto the dance floor with the bride soon after the ceremony. First, the parents were called, then distinguished community members, followed by close relatives and friends, and they in turn were followed by neighbors and town beggars. The groom often joined the dancers, which made for a unique threesome or foursome.

There were other dances featured at east European wedding receptions. If they still exist nowadays the only place to see them is at a Hasidic wedding, both in the United States and Israel. These dances included the *koilich tantz*, in which a woman holding a challah bread and some salt would dance before the bridal couple, wishing them abundance in their new life. The *klapper tantz* was heavy on hand clapping. The *redel, frielichs, karahod* and *hopke* offered the man an opportunity to perform vigorously. A *bezem* dance featured a man and a broom, which was used as a horse or a rifle. In *flash tantz*, a male dancer performed with an open, full bottle of spirits on his head, which despite frenetic dancing somehow managed not to fall and spill. (This bottle dance can still be seen today at Hasidic weddings; often the men who perform it do so while crouching close to the floor, reminiscent of the Cossack dancers.)

Some of the other *shtetl* dances generally not in vogue today include the *bubby's tantz*, the grandmothers' dance; the *mechutaneem tantz*, a dance meant to honor the parents of the bridal couple's parents, who—as a result of their children's marrying—have now become related to each other. There was a *broiges tantz*, during which a man and a woman pretend at first to be angry with each other, and then make up; a *sher*, a *kadril*, a *kazatzky*—Russian, Polish, and Romanian dances that are still occasionally seen today, especially where the bride or groom's parents are relatively new immigrants.

Some Hasidic wedding garb in Europe, in the small hamlets, featured the dancers dressed in peasant costumes, animal skins, or even Cossack uniforms. One of the centuries-old Hasidic dances that may still be seen today at many Orthodox functions features a group of young women, their arms intertwined, who perform before the bride, singing (in Hebrew) "How should one dance before the bride?"—a catchy tune to which many adult guests add rhythmic hand-clapping.

Some Hasidic weddings feature continuous dancing around the groom on the part of his friends, classmates and any male guests who want to enter into the spirit of the moment. In far off Yemen, whose Jewish community was separated from the world's Jews for over one thousand years, the bride was serenaded by professional women singers and dancers.

At the conclusion of the festive wedding meal, an extended grace is recited, containing the same seven bridal blessings that were recited under the canopy.

* * *

How does married life, in Jewish tradition, begin after the wedding? After all, two people who knew each other for many months or even years, have now committed their lives to one another; among other things, this means learning to live with one another as husband and wife. That is probably why traditional Judaism urged the new husband and the new wife to spend a full year with each other—a lengthy period of time in which each spouse would learn to appreciate the other, so that in time each would truly understand the other, and then proceed on life's grand marital adventure.

Realistically, almost no one in these frenzied days can take a year off after the wedding. Somehow, adjustments have to be made. Traditionally Judaism regards the bride and groom for the full year after the wedding as a *chasan* and *kalah*—as bride and groom. During their first year of marriage, it is felt, they should still enjoy the special place that brides and grooms enjoy in society. For those with a romantic bent it is a romantic touch, probably designed to ease the couple's many adjustments.

Religious Jews are required today to spend at least a full week after the wedding in a secluded, honeymoon-like atmosphere, but with spiritual overtones. For the bridal couple, special blessings are pronounced during the first week after the wedding; if the couple find themselves in a public hotel, particularly of course a Jewish-oriented establishment, it is not unusual for the other guests—once they learn that they have a bridal couple in their midst—to surround the pair at their table during a meal and joyously sing with them, and thus help usher them into Jewish family life.

Although modern Israel does not accept this biblical injunction, the Bible does state categorically that a groom may not be drafted into the army during the first year of his marriage, except in a defensive war.

One of the more recent innovations introduced in Conservative and Reform synagogues is for the respective congregations to present the newlyweds with a *mezuzah*, the oblong-shaped casing affixed to the right doorpost (upon entering) which contains a selection from the Bible. Most Jews probably look upon the *mezuzah* as a good luck talisman, but it is really intended to be a reminder that in this Jewish home, the Torah, the Bible, will be taught and observed.

Many Jewish homes greet the bride and groom with bread and salt, signs of peace and prosperity. In parts of

North Africa, notably Libya and the island of Djerba, upon returning from the wedding ceremony, the groom would climb to the roof and drop an earthen pitcher filled with water—and only then would his bride enter the house, walking through the water and broken pottery. Centuries ago, when the Old City of Jerusalem was inhabited by Sephardic Jews almost exclusively, there was an odd custom—a special cake, called a *ruska*, was baked and then broken over the heads of the bridal pair when they returned from their wedding. In Afghanistan, a fowl was slaughtered to celebrate the special, joyous occasion; in what is today the Moslem areas south of Russia, the Jews smeared their doorposts with butter and honey. In Salonika, the large Greek city that once held a substantial number of Jews, the groom would hurry home ahead of his bride, and when she entered the new home he would cast rice and coins at her feet. In Kurdistan, the bride entered the house ahead of her new husband and was given a newborn male infant to hold, while women guests all wished that she too would be blessed with a son.

Nearly all Jewish weddings traditionally took place after the High Holy Days in Libya (which today has a minuscule Jewish population, most of the Jews having fled to Israel). The Libyan Jews who lived in the Atlas mountains combined wedding preparations with foot races, recalling a biblical citation: "He is a bridegroom coming out of his chamber, and rejoices as a strong man to run his course." Oddly, in nearby Tunisia a custom sprang up in which five days after the wedding a competition was held between the new husband and wife. Each was given a knife and told to cut a cooked fish, to be served to company. Traditionally, the groom lost because his knife was blunt while his wife's was sharp.

In some Oriental Jewish communities, some of which still practice the custom of awaiting the groom's bringing out the stained sheet after the wedding, the mother of the bride will hold onto the bedsheet for a long time, just in case someone doubted her daughter's virginity.

According to Jewish religious law, should the bride or groom sustain the loss of a close relative during the first week after the wedding, that week cannot be interrupted. Only after the week is concluded may the requisite sitting of *shiva*—the week-long mourning period—take place.

CHAPTER TWELVE

Jewish Marriage Is Legal, Physical, Emotional, Spiritual

Marriage, in addition to being a union between two people who love each other, and hope to establish a family that in the course of time will include children, is also a contractual, legal joining. It entails certain laws (both civil and religious) and obligations.

In Jewish law, the relationship between husband and wife states:

> Thus, the sages (taught) that a man shall honor his wife more than himself, and shall love her as he loves himself. He shall constantly try to benefit her, according to his means. He shall speak gently with her, and not seek to impose his will over her. Further, he shall be neither sorrowful nor unpredictable. And a wife shall honor her husband without limit and shall accept his authority and abide by his wishes in all her activities.

The marriage contract, the *ketubah*, which dates back from the Middle Ages and is used in almost all wedding ceremonies, is divided into two parts. The first section stipulates the minimum amount of financial support the husband is obligated to pay the wife in the event that he initiates a divorce, or in case he dies before she does, the amount of money his estate is obligated to pay her. The second part makes reference to the dowry which the wife brought to the wedding, and which must be (in part or in whole) returned to her should she be divorced or should her husband pre-decease her. In most communities there is a legal minimum that must be adhered to, so the exact amount is not usually spelled out.

In recent years the Conservative movement in the United States added a clause to the *ketubah* declaring that in the event of a divorce both the husband and the wife agree to appear before a rabbinical court, a *bet din*, and will accept the court's decisions. This was done because in recent years there have been a growing number of civil divorces, with the husband refusing to grant his wife a *get*, a religious divorce, unless (in many cases) she paid him a vast sum of money. Occasionally, it was the woman in a divorce case who refused to grant the religious divorce.

There are tragic cases, particularly in Israel, where a couple separate and the husband refused to grant the wife a religious divorce, not even for a large sum of money. Usually these cases grew out of spite and a deep hate. In such situations, the Israeli rabbis sought to change the man's mind, arguing, cajoling, threatening—and often they succeeded. There have also been extreme situations where a stubborn husband refused all pleas to grant a *get*, and the rabbis quietly called in some husky men to beat him up until he agreed. Such cases are rare, of course, but they do occur. The wives who are left in limbo, neither married nor divorced, while their situations are being worked on, are known as *agunot* (*agunah*, singular), Hebrew for anchored or tethered women.

There recently was an extreme case of a Yemenite Jew considerably older than his wife, who refused all blandishments to divorce her. No amount of pleading on the part of several rabbis could change his mind. The case dragged on for some thirty years; during that time the husband sat in prison, stubbornly refusing her pleas. Finally, he died and the wife of course was now free to remarry, three decades later! To her astonishment and dismay, the rabbis informed her that she was required, as a wife, to recite *kaddish*, the mourners prayer, for him. What she wound up doing remains unknown.

Jewish law stipulates that in getting married, a man has ten "matters" which he is obligated to fulfill vis-a-vis his wife; he also acquires four "rights" against his spouse as a consequence of the marriage. These obligations and rights are not connected to the marriage contract. What's more, the law stresses, it is of no consequence that nothing has been put into writing.

The husband's first two duties to his wife require that he provide her with sustenance and maintenance; these include food, clothes, a home, the necessary furniture, utensils and the like. There is a tradition that a wife "goes up with him but does not descend with him." The wife is to be accorded a standard of living comparable to that of her husband, and that she be maintained in accordance with his means and his social standing. However, if the husband suffers reverses, she is not obligated to reduce her way of life to a standard below that of what she enjoyed just prior to her marriage. Of course, if the marriage is a good one, and the wife chooses to suffer along with her husband and help him get back on his feet, that is another matter.

The husband's third duty to his wife is to satisfy her marital, sexual needs. This the husband must fulfill according to his physical ability. Consideration is extended by the law in this matter to a husband's occupation. For example, if he is at home most of the time and is not required to do heavy, manual labor, he must satisfy his wife's needs every day. But if he is, for example, a seaman away from home for long stretches of time, his obligation to cohabit with his wife is limited to the time he is home. On the other hand, if a husband is unable to fulfill his obligation to his wife because of some physical impairment, she is entitled to demand a divorce—unless there are reasonable prospects for his recovery at an early date.

The fourth obligation for the husband states that in the event of the marriage's end, either by death or divorce, he is required to pay all the expenses enumerated in the marriage contract.

Obligation number five declares that the husband must pay all his wife's medical expenses in the event of her infirmity.

Obligation number six refers to a criminal act that was carried out throughout the Middle Ages: kidnapping for ransom. In the event of his wife's being kidnapped, the husband is required to pay the ransom in order to obtain his wife's release.

The husband's seventh duty deals with the eventuality of her death, in which case he is obligated to arrange for her burial according to Jewish law, and to pay all expenses connected with the interment and with the erection of a suitable tombstone.

The eighth and ninth obligations of the husband have to do with arrangements that he must make for the care of his widow and their minor daughters, in the event of his demise. (In Jewish law, the sons, and their sons, inherit the father's estate, which is why special provisions were made for the daughters. If the father who died was poor and left no real assets, the community was expected to assume responsibility for the widow and her children, until such time as the widow remarried and the children grew up and no longer need communal support.)

The tenth and final obligation of the husband says that if his wife pre-deceases him, the dowry she brought to the marriage and the wife's vested financial interests in the marriage contract would be transferred to the sons of that marriage.

The rights that the husband acquires in the marriage are: first, his wife's handiwork; second, should she find something of value, it belongs to the husband; third, some of the wife's property, given to her exclusively, comes under the husband's stewardship with the understanding that in the event of the marriage's dissolution, the husband must restore the value of that property to her; fourth, property which belongs to the wife solely must remain hers alone, except that the husband may enjoy the fruits thereof. Here too in the event of the dissolution of the marriage, the husband must return the wife's private property. If its value rose during the period of their marriage, he must pay the additional amount.

Nonetheless, if the wife dies before the husband, he inherits all of her assets; even her children are not entitled to anything left by their mother. These ancient religious laws and attitudes are certainly not in keeping with society's current views, in the majority of cases. The laws of the state in which people live today that deal with inheritance and similar matters override all other religious laws and traditions.

If a wife refuses to cohabit with her husband, for a least twelve months, she is call a *moredet*, a rebel. In this event, the husband is not required to provide her with maintenance and he may divorce her summarily. Under such circumstances he is not obligated to return to her any of the benefits in the marriage contract that she would otherwise be entitled to receive.

CHAPTER THIRTEEN

Divorce and Childlessness: Ancient Issues

A marriage, Jewish laws stipulates, may be terminated either by a divorce, or the death of one of the partners. If a spouse dies, a widower may remarry after conclusion of the three biblical-pilgrim holidays (Passover, Shavuot, and Sukkot), which fall generally in April, June and September. If, however, the father-spouse has small children in need of a mother's care, he may remarry after a month of mourning. A widow, on the other hand, is not permitted to remarry for three months after her husband's death, so as to avoid any doubt about paternity should her remarriage produce a child.

If a husband or a wife dies, the testimony of one witness is ample to establish that fact; in most other cases, two witnesses are needed. If it is the wife who dies, the husband inherits her estate, but he is required to pay her children the value of the marriage contract upon his death. His own children from a previous marriage do not possess any claim to this contractual obligation.

In a question of divorce, the ancient biblical law seems to be stacked in favor of the husband. He can, if he wishes, "write a bill of divorce and give it in her hand, and send her out of his house, and (the wife) departs from his house and becomes another man's wife," if she "finds no favor in his eyes" or "because he has found some unseemly thing in her." On the other hand, he cannot summarily divorce her if he had accused her falsely of not being a virgin when he married her, or if the marriage came about as a result of his having raped her.

In all of the Bible, there are no narratives of men divorcing their wives freely. Father Abraham, regarded as the first Jew, hesitated and stalled when Sarah, his wife, demanded that he send away ("divorce") his concubine, Hagar. When Paltiel was forced to surrender the beautiful Michal, he shed tears. And when Ezra the scribe, upon the return to the Jewish homeland of the Israelites from Babylonian captivity, demanded that they send away their non-Jewish wives, many resisted.

Ideally, marriage is a lifelong, permanent partnership. The Bible puts it strongly: "Therefore, a man shall leave his father and his mother, and shall cleave to his wife, and they shall be one flesh." The one cause that traditionally did lead to divorce, more so in the past than in modern times, was if the marriage failed to result in children. After ten years of marriage, and the wife's inability to give birth was regarded as conclusive, the husband had the right to divorce her and marry another.

There were many causes of course in times gone by and even more so in our generation when a barren couple ignored the divorce ruling, and either lived their lives without children or adopted other people's children and raised them as their own.

When World War II ended, fairly large numbers of barren Jewish couples sought to adopt orphaned Jewish children after the Holocaust; some succeeded, but most did not because the numbers of such surviving children were so few.

In the final years of the twentieth century, it has become quite customary to see Jewish couples who apparently could not have children of their own attending synagogue services with their adopted youngsters—many of whom have Oriental backgrounds, or children from extremely poor families in Latin America or eastern Europe.

In ancient times, the lot of a divorced woman was very difficult. Usually following a divorce, she returned to her parents' home, leaving the children, if there were any, with her former husband. Apparently, if the children were very young she could take them with her until they were weaned. By the age of six, her sons were required by law to return to their father's house.

A divorcee by Jewish law is free to remarry, but she may not marry a *kohen*, a member of the priestly tribe. This ruling is still observed in Orthodox families, and probably also in much of the Conservative world; the Reform wing of Judaism pays it no heed. Most people whose family names are Cohen (or an adaptation such as Kahan, Kagan, Kohen, Kohansky etc.) and often Kaplan are descended from the priestly tribe. At synagogue services, a *kohen* is the first to be called for the honor of standing by the Torah, where the holy scroll is read aloud.

The two thousand rabbis and biblical commentators whose views and interpretations are recorded in the Talmud agreed with the basic provisos handed down about divorce, but they made serious efforts to slow down the process so that husbands would not act rashly. The *get* that the husband had to hand his wife, the rabbis said, had to be written and delivered within certain precise parameters. Indeed the marriage contract itself was instituted so that the "daughters of Israel should not be easy in the eyes of their husbands to divorce." The talmudic amendments to the divorce law of the Bible added a very important element: a man could not divorce his wife unilaterally; if the wife refused to accept the divorce, the husband could not merely hand it to her as a court summons. In other words, both sides have to agree. This ruling on divorce is in force to this day.

A Jewish religious court, a *bet din*, is sometimes called into a case where there is disagreement between the spouses on the question of divorce. The court can listen to both sides, advise both sides, express a view—but the court cannot forcibly cause a divorce. Only a husband's giving of a kosher *get* to his wife, and her acceptance of it, can do that. In a Jewish divorce case, unlike in most civil courts, no special grounds are required to sue for divorce such as accusations of adultery; if both parties are in agreement, a divorce will follow. What's more, nowadays, unlike in ancient times, a wife as well as a husband can initiate a divorce.

The only time a religious court in Israel, where the court has sole juridical power, can impose a fine on one of the parties, or even imprison a recalcitrant spouse, is if the spouse refuses to cooperate with the other partner out of spite or because of greed vis-a-vis a potential settlement.

The jailing of a husband for refusing to give his wife a *get* until he receives an outlandish sum of money has become a fairly common occurrence in Israel. Sometimes a husband simply takes off, leaving his wife in limbo. After a certain amount of time, the rabbinical authorities in Israel will send a special representative to try to find him; once found, he must then be persuaded to grant his wife the *get* so that she can go forward with her life and remarry.

What happens, however, if the recalcitrant party is the wife? And she refuses her husband a *get*?

Here too there is a solution, albeit not an easy one to obtain. This example is based on an actual event: a Jewish couple in Israel, with children, had marital problems and decided to divorce. The husband wanted the divorce more than the wife. The divorce machinery was activated, and in the course of time, before the *get* could be prepared to be handed to the wife, she disappeared from Israel, winding up in a European country. There she met and married a local Jew, after having obtained a local civil divorce. The husband, in Israel, after a time met and wished to marry an Israeli woman, a divorcee. However, now he needed a *get*. When he turned to his ex-wife, she refused. When he asked her why, since she was now remarried and presumably happy, her answer was, just because!

The husband now turned to the Israeli rabbinate and explained his predicament. They told him that if everything he said was true, he could still obtain a *get* by having one hundred ordained, certified rabbis sign a petition attesting to the wife's behavior, and granting him a special dispensation religious divorce.

With the help of a rabbi-friend, the husband went calling on rabbis who lived in an Orthodox community; soon enough he had his one hundred rabbinical signatures. He and his intended got married and presumably are living happily ever after.

The most common grounds for instituting divorce proceedings today are when either the husband or the wife refuses to cohabit, or when either party has a physical defect that precludes co-habitation—which the other spouse did not know about prior to the wedding. If either spouse knew about the defect, serious enough to prevent sexual union, and proceeded with the marriage anyway, a *get* cannot be granted.

When a properly-written *get* is presented to a wife, she then hands it to the religious court. The judges ascertain that the *get* is strictly kosher, tear the document in half, and file it in that form: They then hand a document to the wife, stating that according to Jewish law she is divorced.

The laws of divorce in Jewish tradition are numerous and complex, and require specially-trained rabbis to execute correctly. Generally speaking, the rabbis of old felt that by slowing up and complicating the divorce procedure, they might obliquely persuade some couples from going ahead with this difficult and traumatic step. God, in Jewish tradition, is regarded as the Grand Matchmaker. Thus, when a divorce takes place, "even the altar sheds tears."

The problem of the *agunah*, the woman whose husband disappeared in war or who simply vanished, is still a source of great sorrow. At the turn of the century, when thousands of Jewish immigrants poured into the United States from eastern Europe, many of the husbands came on their own first, planning to work hard, save some money, and then send for their spouses and children. While this was often the case, unfortunately, it was not a sure thing. Sometimes the husband in his loneliness met another woman, fell in love, or maybe discovered that she was rich, and took off with her to start life anew. Thus, by abandoning his wife in Europe, he produced another *agunah*, a woman in limbo who was not free to marry according to Jewish law.

During the first few decades of the twentieth century, the major New York Yiddish dailies, notably *The Forward*, ran pictures and stories about these runaway husbands, asking readers to turn them in and earn a *mitzvah*, a good deed. Obviously there were some cases of an innocent Jewish woman in America who married in good faith, believing that her husband was an eligible bachelor, only to discover through the Yiddish paper that he was really a runaway husband who had a wife and children stranded in Russia or Poland.

In both biblical and modern times in Israel, Jewish soldiers going off to war wrote a conditional *get*, i.e., in the event of their death, their wives were released from the marital bond and were free to remarry.

Interestingly, American soldiers preparing to enter war-torn Bosnia in the Balkans in the final years of the twentieth century were encouraged by their commanders to write their wills, which presumably would include a proviso that their wives were free to remarry in the event of their death.

* * *

Jewish tradition always taught that it was important for a potential husband or wife not to "set your eyes on beauty, set your eyes on family."

Yichus, a family's background in terms of scholarship, ethical behavior and religious observance, was always regarded with far greater respect and even awe than mere material achievements. Until the year 70 C.E., when the Second Temple was destroyed by the Romans, careful records were kept of the priestly family's genealogy. Such genealogical standards no longer prevail, but even today one can read about the forthcoming wedding of a son of one famous Hasidic rabbi and the daughter of another—scions who presumably will carry on centuries-old Jewish traditions.

Jewish law is very clear on certain practices: incest, sodomy, homosexuality and bestiality are forbidden; the latter three are seen as capital offenses. Lesbianism was not mentioned in the Bible, but it is prohibited in talmudic law and is punishable by flogging.

CHAPTER FOURTEEN

Forbidden Unions—When a Marriage Never Happened

Jewish religious law declares that intercourse between a Jew and a non-Jew is forbidden. If such a union produces a child, the child follows the religion of the mother; if the mother is Jewish, the child even under these circumstances is regarded as a full-fledged Jew.

Incest is not only a strictly forbidden transgression in Jewish law, but even "approaching" any person with whom such intercourse is prohibited is not allowed, under penalty of death. Kissing and embracing such a person is seen as pre-coital activity and is barred by Jewish law; if it is done, the sinner must be flogged as punishment. However, kissing a mother or an aunt or a sister, who normally do not arouse sexual responses, is acceptable.

Other acts that are stringently prohibited include indecent gestures or hints to women with whom sexual relations are not allowed; being alone with a woman with whom intercourse is not allowed (except a mother, daughter or a menstruating wife); making love with one's wife in public view. If a man finds himself in a secluded place with a woman married to another man, no punishment is called for, the rabbis taught, explaining that if she were to be flogged in public her reputation would be sorely damaged.

Certain categories of marriage are not permitted: Between a Jew and a non-Jewish partner; between a man and a woman who is already married; and any of the incestuous unions banned in the Bible. There are categories of marriage that are considered valid but nonetheless prohibited, e.g., if a man marries the former wife of his father's brother; it does not matter if they are half-brothers. Such prohibited but valid marriages oddly do not require a religious divorce because the marriage was regarded as totally unacceptable; it is as though it never took place. In the case where a man marries an already married woman (presumably she hid her status from the second husband), the law requires that both husbands divorce her.

In recent years a number of Reform rabbis have officiated at weddings where one partner is Jewish and the other is not. The rationale here is that Judaism should reach out to the non-Jewish partner and over a period of time persuade him or her to formally convert to Judaism. While many Reform rabbis still oppose this practice; there are also a very small number who will co-officiate at such an intermarriage. Needless to say, the Orthodox and Conservative wings of Judaism consider such practices anathema.

Jewish tradition generally is more lenient in its attitude to married men who have extramarital affairs, although such activities are strictly banned. However if a married woman, of her own free will, agrees to have sexual relations with a man other than her husband, and she is found out, she and her husband may never again indulge in love-making. This does not apply if she was raped, except if her husband is a *kohen*, a member of the priestly tribe. In that case, she and her husband are prohibited to each other.

If a woman is divorced, and then remarries, and if her second marriage ends either by death or divorce, she and her first husband may not marry each other again. A divorced woman may not marry a *kohen*, even if after remarriage her husband died and she became widowed. And a *kohen* may not remarry his own former wife, following an earlier divorce.

There is a very small sect of Jews known as Karaites who essentially follow the laws of the Bible but do not accept the Oral Law, i.e., the talmudic amendments and additions that make up a large part of Jewish religious law. Their divorce laws are considered very lax, and children born to a divorced Karaite couple are generally regarded as *mamzerim* by the mainstream religious leaders; therefore, marriage of a Karaite with a non-Karaite Jew is usually discouraged, lest the union be forbidden in Jewish law.

Customarily a marriage between two brothers and their intended spouses or two sisters with their spouses is not allowed to take place on the same day. The feeling here is that the joyousness of one wedding should not diminish from the happiness of the other.

*   *   *

Although the Bible does not forbid a man from having more than one wife at a time, monogamy in ancient, as well as in modern times, was and is the Jewish practice. Even a cursory reading of the book of Psalms or the book of Proverbs demonstrates that monogamy was considered as the ideal state of marriage. Virtually all of the biblical prophets, when they spoke of God and His spouse, the Jewish people, used a metaphor of one husband and one wife. When Christianity came upon the scene, some two millennia ago, it transferred this precept from Judaism to its own faith.

During talmudic times, however, a limited amount of polygamy did exist. Some 1,000 years ago it was officially and formally banned in Ashkenazic communities; most Sephardic communities eventually followed suit. One ancient rabbi taught that a man "may marry several women, on condition that he can provide for them." The talmudic sages also said that a man should not marry more than four wives. This may be the source of the Muslim teaching that permits a man to marry four wives simultaneously. Historians have theorized that in the Sephardic communities of North Africa and Spain, polygamy persisted for many years owing to local economic conditions. An unmarried woman in those times was not only in dire financial straits but her life was in peril without a husband to protect her.

The ban promulgated about one thousand years ago against polygamy stated that a Jew could not marry more than one wife unless he obtained a special dispensation signed by one hundred rabbis. What's more the rabbis had to come from three different countries. This ban, known as the *herem d'Rabbenu Gershom*, also forbade a husband from divorcing his wife against her will.

Until monogamy was firmly established in Sephardic communities, many Sephardic rabbis inserted into the marriage contract a clause stipulating that the husband could not take a second wife without the first wife's permission.

*　*　*

Virtually the entire Ethiopian Jewish community was evacuated to Israel in a miraculous rescue operation in the final years of the 1980s. It is doubtful that the Ethiopian Jews now being integrated into their new lives in Israel will continue to observe the ancient customs and traditions that they practiced when they were a minority in Ethiopia, but it is certainly interesting to remember their unusual marital mores.

For centuries when a seventeen-year-old youth and a nine-year-old girl were regarded as marriageable, the parents of the two young people would start making plans for their marriage by dispatching a male relative to the home of the girl and formally asking that she be given in marriage to the young male relation, although the actual wedding date was generally set for three years later when she reached at least the age of twelve.

If the proposal was accepted, the girl's father would give the young man's representative a coin, sealing the agreement. If the girl's father rejected the proposal, no money was offered. Most weddings among the Jews of Ethiopia were held on Sunday or Monday. On the evening of the day before the wedding the young bride is brought to the groom's home where relatives and friends gather to recite prayers; the *kes*, the Ethiopian Jews' priest, beats a drum, and a colored thread is tied around the groom's forehead. Later, the groom is accompanied to the bride's home by his attendants, where he spends the night.

On the following day the bride is carried into the young husband's home by relatives from both sides. If it is then ascertained that the bride was a virgin, all the wedding guests bless her and announce that fact joyously. However, if it is determined that she was not a virgin, the husband removes the thread from his forehead, goes to the chief *kes*, and notifies him that his wife had lost her virginity before she came to the bridal chamber. At this point, the marriage is declared null and void by the high priest, and no member of the Ethiopian community is permitted to marry her.

Traditionally, an Ethiopian wedding, replete with singing and dancing and feasting would continue right through for more than a week, although festivities were suspended on the Sabbath.

* * *

In the Caucasus, in what used to be the southern region of the Soviet Union, where Jews have lived since the destruction of the Second Temple by the Romans in the year 70 C.E., and where many Jews disappeared into the general Muslim population during recent centuries through coerced conversion, weddings took place on Wednesday. Customarily, a week before the wedding ceremony, a few young female relatives of the bride would don her clothes, and keep her company until the appointed day of the ceremony arrived. The groom, on the day of the ceremony, would send gifts of meat, rice and flour to the bride-to-be and her guests. The latter traditionally would take the rice flour and sprinkle it on the heads of young people gathered outside the bride's home, while the groom-to-be prepares a festive meal for his friends.

On the morning of the Sabbath, the bride's friends went from home to home extending invitations to the forthcoming wedding, and the invitees responded by offering the inviters all kinds of food staples, such as sugar, coffee, apples and eggs.

At the Sabbath synagogue service the groom is not called to the Torah—as is done in Ashkenazic families—prior to the wedding. Instead he is honored at the Torah when it is read aloud after the formal wedding ceremony takes place.

Immediately following the wedding, all the guests accompany the couple first to the home of the groom, and then to the bride's home; in each place the guests are served festive meals, accompanied by music furnished by young girls playing the harmonica and trumpet. Both the groom and the bride, on the Sabbath following the wedding and on the following day, host all their guests with additional festive meals; instead of instrumental music, now the young girls offer local vocal compositions. Oddly, the bride now dresses in mourning garments, to show her sorrow at the fact that she is leaving the home of her parents.

On the day before the actual wedding, both the bride and groom fast. Some time in the afternoon, the couple, accompanied by their relatives, are escorted to the sea where they bathe; afterwards they don their special bridal clothes. On the return from the sea, the couple is accompanied by young people singing, clapping and beating on drums. While the bride's hair—still wet from these—is being combed and dried, she kneels before her mother, who blesses her. She is then escorted to the wedding site, accompanied by her brothers, or if she has none, by an uncle.

The groom is returned from the sea accompanied by his friends, and by girls who offer him candy dishes, as well as a tree branch on which hang silken handkerchiefs and coins. At his home, all the women present kiss the groom's forehead and he is blessed by all his relatives. He then proceeds to the synagogue's courtyard, escorted by music-playing friends where the rabbi awaits both him and his bride. The wedding canopy is ready, and the groom steps under it, awaiting his new wife.

At the bride's home, her parents mourn the imminent

loss of their daughter. Finally, the bride arrives, as do both sets of parents and all the invited guests, and the ceremony begins. In the Caucasian rite, both the rabbi and the groom sit on chairs under the wedding canopy holding wine glasses, while the bride walks around her husband-to-be a number of times. Both the rabbi and groom remain seated during the ceremony, drinking after each blessing.

When the ceremony is over, guests shoot off guns and rockets. The bride, who is tightly veiled, mounts a horse and is led by her attendants and the groom's relatives to her new home. The accompanying guests who walk along shower her with rice, a fertility symbol. Young women guests dance and sing until the bride crosses into her new home, when they smear the doorposts with honey. A few more shots are discharged into the air; the musicians who walked alongside the horse are paid off, and the wedding procession is concluded.

CHAPTER FIFTEEN

Marriage: A Cure for What Ails You?

Why get married?

In the closing years of the 1990s, far more than in any other period in history, eligible young men and women are asking themselves, Why marry? And indeed, acting on their own questions, many choose non-traditional forms of a relationship. There is "trial marriage," "open marriage," cohabitation without marriage, and other forms bringing men and women together outside the boundaries of legal, traditional marriage.

Presumably those who opt for these lifestyles are looking for happiness but they do not wish to be "burdened" by the strict rules and regulations that are part and parcel of getting married.

Society as a whole is suffering from some kind of malaise which manifests itself in loneliness, unhappiness, unfulfillment. Psychologists, psychiatrists and other people and institutions dealing with mental or emotional health are busy. Divorce rates are skyrocketing. A young, well-adjusted couple married and truly in love is becoming more and more rare; as time goes on, the same can be said of older couples.

For Jews who care deeply or even just a little about the future and the continuity of the Jewish people, there is an extra dimension here. A young Jew who chooses not to marry a fellow Jew and raise a traditional Jewish family must know, deep in his or her heart, that the decision is adding to the steady corrosion of the Jewish people. The Jewish community cannot continue and remain viable if the Jewish family ceases to exist. True, there are some Jews who believe that the quiet, peaceful demise of the Jewish people through intermarriage and integration would be a good thing, and finally put an end to the disease called anti-Semitism. But in all likelihood most Jews, old and young, those without a strong Jewish education and those with, instinctively feel that the disappearance of the Jewish people from the world's stage—after nearly 4,000 years—would be a calamity for all mankind.

Judaism has always taught that an unmarried person is an incomplete person; such an individual lives for himself or herself instead of reaching out to a fellow human being, a basic component of being a fulfilled human being.

Rabbi Reuven P. Bulka, a psychologist as well as a congregational rabbi (in Canada), has said: "The creation model figures prominently in the matter of 'Why marry?' The original human being, Adam, was of two forms, one male, the other female. These two components were separated by God's surgical procedure, and the two, male and female, in coming together effectively return to the oneness that is their pristine state."

Marriage, in the Bible, is thus projected as the natural human condition.

> Marriage is an ideal that has no age limit. One should
> marry even in the twilight years, when childbearing might

no longer be possible but value-sharing is still very much attainable. A good marriage, in which one partner cares deeply for the other, is the firmament for *hesed*, for kindness, concern, empathy and warmth.

We do not worry that through concern for the other we may lose our individuality, our sense of who we are. Devotion to our partner in marriage is the way we emulate God and uncover our divine image. We achieve completeness not by turning inward, but by focusing outward.

Rabbi Bulka tackles the eternal question confronting young men and women: *Who shall I marry?* He says:

We would like the right partner to fall into our lap, like manna from heaven… we look for divine signals… that this indeed will be a marriage made in heaven. But we do not really know; we hope, but we are not sure. What is clear is that we usually mate with someone we deserve, because who we are impacts on the person we desire to marry. And how each spouse grows after marriage affects how the other will develop and how the marriage will grow.

It is generally true that we derive from marriage what we put into it, (but) there are some basic features that increase the chances for a good marriage. Physical attractiveness is one such ingredient… (it) is vital. We certainly should take this factor into account when choosing a mate…the prospective partner's height and age should be given serious consideration.

Important as the physical component may be, however, it is not primary. A physically beautiful partner who is not compatible in other ways is a poor marriage choice… a person's inner beauty is much more crucial to a marriage than external good looks. Kindness, sensitivity, and responsibility are paramount in a marriage. Brazenness and arrogance are not noble traits...we must avoid those who manifest them.

Does this then mean that people who display conceit and insolence should not marry? Rabbi Bulka believes that such people "have no business marrying." A prospective marital partner who insists on marrying only someone with good traits is practicing a "form of genetic engineering" and thus weeds out those traits which are inconsistent with Judaism's teaching, Bulka says. Thus, "emphasis must be placed on the family from which our prospective mate comes" for "families are the breeding ground for our values," he adds. Bulka warns however that there is no guarantee that "good parents have good children," but it is more likely.

*   *   *

Deciding to get married is a major step in life. Of course, it should not be a negative decision, i.e., so as to avoid an unpleasant situation in which one finds oneself, but a decision taken only for all the right and positive reasons. The prime requisite in deciding to take the marital step is maturity. One must reach a point where one understands that life is not only fun and games. Marriage means sharing with and being responsible for one's life partner, and for the children that may follow. There must be a genuine understanding on the part of both potential marriage partners that the step they embark upon, after the brief ceremony under the wedding canopy, will entail hard work for the new family unit to come together and function smoothly as one. Inevitably, there will be crises and hard times, as well as peaks of joy and gratification— and one must be ready for whatever lies in store.

On the pragmatic and "unromantic" side, there must be a clear understanding on the part of both partners of the means needed to sustain the marriage. If such mundane questions are not broached before a couple gets married, then the lack of adequate financial support for the tiny new family can imperil its viability. When a couple is genuinely mature and has gotten to know one another over a suitable period of time, and if it is evident to both the man and the woman that they seem to have every chance to establish a happy and financially stable family, there is no reason to delay their planned marriage.

On the other hand, if one or both of the partners seem to be seriously questioning the step they are about to take, it is wise that they retreat, think hard, and not plunge into what may turn out to be a sea of dangerous rocks.

Each partner in a forthcoming marriage must be truly knowledgeable of the contemplated major step in their lives, must be absolutely sure they want to spend their life together with the other partner, have and raise children—and thus be a source of joy to their families and a source of strength for the Jewish community.

* * *

What then is the magic formula for a happy marriage?

The author Francine Klagsbrun writes that there is no formula, but "there are certain abilities and outlooks that couples in strong marriages have—not all of them at all times—but a large proportion a good part of the time...they fall into eight categories." These, she says, are:

> An ability to change and tolerate change. An ability to live with the unchangeable. An assumption of permanence. Trust. A balance of dependence. An enjoyment of each other. A cherished and shared history. And last but certainly not least—Luck.

Just like in life, Klagsbrun writes, change is inevitable in marriage.

Children are born, they go off to school, they leave home. Spouses age, get sick, drop old interests, take on new ones, make new friends... parents get old and die, couples move from apartments to homes and back to apartments, from one town to another. Partners become involved in work and pull back from work. Changes bring anxieties and disequilibrium, (but) in the strongest marriages (partners) are able to adapt to change that is happening in the marriage or in the other partner and, when called for, to change themselves.

Touching on the fast-moving events of the last decades of the twentieth century, Klagsbrun says, couples were confronted with vast changes from the time that many of them first married.

Marriage had a set form, when husbands knew that their work was to provide for the family and wives knew that theirs was to care for the home and children... the world turned upside down, marriage was ridiculed as a dying if not dead institution. Husbands (were now told they were) insensitive and dictatorial, and their wives were oppressed in stifling marriages. A new emphasis (came) on a woman's right to seek her own work outside the home and on a man's responsibility to shift some of his energies and time away from the outside to his home and his family. The changes brought chaos to many marriages that found all the premises on which they had been built cut out from under them.... People who stay happily married see themselves not as victims of fate but as free agents who make choices in life.... They are open to changing themselves, pulling away from what *was* in order to make what *is* alive and vital.

And yet on the other hand, there are times in a marriage when a spouse recognizes that the partner in the marriage has an unresolved conflict, and accepts it. Couples who have been married a long time and who have submitted to some probing generally reply, when asked for the secret of their long marriage, "We don't expect perfection." They explain that the marital partner has certain characteristics that they would prefer did not exist, but all the other good traits outweigh that particular weakness—and they have learned to accept it and live with it.

In other words, these spouses focus on the good aspects of their marriage and to the best of their ability shunt aside those things they dislike in their spouse.

In these fast-moving days, the ideal of marital permanence may seem to some a bit of an anachronism, but it is a very important factor in the philosophy and thinking of long and happily-married couples. Each marriage partner is totally committed to the marriage as a sacred, permanent institution, as well as to each other. These long-married couples see in marriage a stabilizing Rock of Gibraltar in their lives that gives them a strong faith in who they are, and imbues them with a strong sense of confidence.

Although the term "trust" may seem to some people an old-fashioned word, it is really an extremely important foundation for a happy and long-lasting marriage. "The trust that lies at the heart of a happy marriage," Klagsbrun writes, "is also the foundation for sexual enjoyment among partners. When mates speak about sexual loving, they almost always speak about trusting feelings that had expanded over the years... trust is also the reason invariably given for a commitment to monogamy. 'I may be tempted,' one spouse commented, 'but I wouldn't want to violate our trust.' ... Trust is regarded by many couples as the linchpin of their marriage."

In the best of marriages, writes Klagsbrun, "partners are mutually dependent... they are aware of their dependencies and not ashamed to cater to them, acknowledging openly their debt to one another."

Partners in established, traditional marriages—as well as mates in non-traditional relationships—share emotional dependencies. The dependencies between husband and wife, usually, go back and forth in a marriage, each supporting the other; over a period of time, a "balance" is developed, which helps keep the marriage strong and stable.

It is important to stress that this strong inter-dependent feeling certainly does not mean obliterating one's spouse's individual personality by the other. Quite the contrary, it is important for husbands and wives throughout the marriage to emphasize the individuality of each partner. In other words, each partner must feel worthy of his or her own self, without feeling a need to link their sense of self-esteem to the partner's personality.

A basic requirement for a happy and long marriage is that each spouse genuinely enjoys the company of the other. Each partner not only loves each other but really likes each other, for they, after a period of time, become each other's best friend. If the two of them can spend a quiet evening at home together, and can honestly say they enjoy just being in the company of the other, that is a very good sign of a strong marriage. Of course they can also spend the evening, or any other part of the day, conversing; and, lo and behold, somehow they always have something interesting to say to one another—something provocative, amusing, intimate, insightful, almost as though they were dating after a few weeks rather than having been married for many years.

If two spouses pursue two different areas of interest they nevertheless exchange ideas that reflect a common value system. One spouse, let us say the husband, may be a financial corporate vice-president and the wife may be a kindergarten teacher; if there is genuine love between them, and they share the same basic values, they will be able to discuss not only the events of the day but also the events of their own working day.

After having been married a number of years, most couples can recognize when their partners, at a social function, will recount a favorite story. And they really don't mind, for their love for the spouse is so great and meaningful that hearing the same story repeatedly does not matter. After many years of marriage, most couples have developed a storehouse of favorite family anecdotes that bind them, and them alone.

Husbands and wives who can remember together their years of dating, the arrival of children, the joy that each spouse has given each other, the special parental pleasure they shared from their children, the sorrows they shared and comforted one another with—these are all very special memories that no one in any part of the world has except them. And this exclusivity of shared memories is a very strong and special source of strength to each of them, and to the two of them together.

So, as in many other aspects of life, in marriage too one needs that old-fashioned ingredient, *luck*—or *mazel*. You can't buy it, you can't order it from a catalogue, you can't tell your secretary—or your parents—to get hold of it for you.

When you choose a life partner in that great adventure called marriage, in addition to all the other components, one is blessed if in addition to all other factors, one has luck.

One more observation is important. A happily-married, loving couple needs some time and some space in private. Two people, no matter how much they are devoted to each other, need to hear other voices and exchange ideas with other people; they need time to think, to relax, to reinforce one's sense of self. Inevitably, this private, personal time strengthens the marital relationship, and enhances both spouses.

This does *not* mean that either the husband or the wife should go on vacation alone; that's a formula that could lead to trouble.

But if one or two evenings a week are spent separately, he for example, at a meeting or a lecture in which his wife is not interested, and she at an education forum or a philanthropic gathering—these small separations seem to be very salutary.

As the spouses hurry home, after a few hours away from their partners, in most cases they will subconsciously know that the person waiting for them at home is their very special *zivig*, their heaven-directed life partner.

CHAPTER SIXTEEN

So, What's the Secret Formula for Married Bliss?

Jewish tradition teaches that in matters of marriage, parents can give a dowry—but not good luck. When the wife is a queen, Judaism says, the husband is a king. When an old maid marries, she is transformed into a young wife. When a man marries, Jewish tradition says, he gives a marriage certificate to his wife—and a bill of divorce to his mother. The Divine Presence hovers over every bride. A *shadchan*—a marriage broker—must of necessity be a liar; but God does not punish the *shadchan* for telling lies. A man without a wife is like a *lulav* (a branch of the date palm) without an *etrog* (a citron). To fulfill the holiday of *Sukkot* ritual, both are needed, and they must be held and prayed over in unison.

*   *   *

So, is there no way to ensure a happy marriage? Is it a matter of luck, guesswork, chance? The tradition that God

Himself is busy in heaven arranging marriages is lovely, but how realistic is it, when the divorce rate is so high? And when couples separate, fight, desert one another, have affairs, in what seems a mad, even zany quest for the magical formula that will guarantee their "happiness"—what then? When a son, or even a daughter, breaks up a family, abandoning children, or seeing them as a "visitation" parent, and the grandparents excuse this action with the trite comment, "Well, so long as he/she is happy," we must conclude that something very wrong is afoot.

This quest for the secret formula for true bliss is, of course, not new. In biblical times, the ancient Israelites believed quite literally that God busied Himself with matchmaking. In the book of Proverbs, it is written quite clearly: "The home and riches are the inheritance of fathers, but a prudent wife is from the Lord." To this day, when a groom comes to the synagogue on the Sabbath following his wedding, in the Sephardic tradition, the service includes the selection from Genesis, in which the story of Isaac's marriage to Rebecca is narrated, as a perfect example of a providentially-ordained marriage.

In the modern Jewish wedding ceremony, during the recitation of the Seven Benedictions, one of the chanted blessings reminds all listeners that God has made man in His image, and in the creation of Eve, God said: "I will make for man a helpmate unto him." Thus, Jewish teaching says, the bride was fashioned in heaven.

Even Shakespeare, in Henry V, declared: "God, the best maker of all marriages, combine your hearts in one."

The moral is quite simple: If the bride or the groom, prior to the wedding, does not truly feel that the impending marriage does not have a touch of heavenly blessing, perhaps the wedding should be postponed or even cancelled. A good, happy marriage must include a sense of divine guidance. A Yiddish folk song popular a half-century ago describes a groom waxing rhapsodic about his forthcoming wife-to-be:

Shain vee dee l'vonah (Beautiful as the moon),

Lichtig vee dee shteren (Lustrous as the stars),

Fun himmel a matoneh (From Heaven, a gift)

Bist du mir tsu'geshikt (You were sent to me).

Anthropologists and sociologists have concluded that marriage is humanity's oldest social institution. It arose, as does marriage today, in response to profoundly elementary biological instincts. As Rabbi Sidney Goldstein put it, "marriage also rests upon an economic basis—in every stage of civilization, marriage makes it possible for men and women to provide themselves with food, shelter and protection that would be more difficult if they lived apart."

Goldstein continues: "Marriage, in the course of time, has come to possess a legal basis; it is incorporated into the code of law of every nation. It not only imposes responsibilities upon both husband and wife but also legally guarantees privileges and rights that neither must deny. Likewise, marriage, we have come to learn, rests on a psychological basis. Men and women are both moved by desires, yearnings and aspirations that marriage meets more adequately than any other relationship. That is probably the reason that the rabbinical proverb arose, 'A man without a wife is not a complete person.' All these aspects of marriage have persisted to our own time; it is unwise to ignore any of them."

However, Goldstein cautioned, "We are living in an aggressively secular period... it is dangerous that men and women, especially young people will interpret marriage in nothing more than scientific or secular terms." These secularists, especially the young among them, claim that marriage is nothing more than a biological device to perpetuate the human species; or some will argue that marriage is no more than a civil contract that two people make, and they should be free, when they wish, to dissolve that agreement."

Agreeing that marriage rests partly on biological, economic, legal, social and psychological basis, Goldstein says: "According to Judaism's teachings, marriage is more than a biological mating, more than an economic partnership, more than a social institution, more than a legal institution, more even than a psychological association. In Judaism, the term for marriage is *kiddushin*, derived from the Hebrew word *kadosh*, which means "holy." Thus, as Judaism sees it, marriage is a consecration, or a sanctification of life itself. Its primary purpose is to add a dimension of holiness to the newlyweds, a holiness that will characterize all the years of their marriage. When the bride and groom stand under the wedding canopy, and the rabbi calls on the groom to slip the wedding band on his bride's finger, he says, loud and clear: *Ha'rai at m'koodeshet lee k'dat Moshe v'Yysrael, b'taba'at zu* (You are consecrated unto me, according to the laws of Moses and Israel, by means of this ring).

The key word in this brief but so powerful ceremony is *consecrated*. From that point on, the bride and the groom will become husband and wife and will conduct themselves with an added dimension: holiness. As Rabbi Goldstein says:

> Marriage at its highest is a spiritual relationship sanctioned by society and sanctified by religion. When marriage attains these heights, it stirs from their sleep elemental impulses that run back through the ages... it clothes the man and woman it touches with a garment of golden light.... Those who marry and live together in this

spirit know intuitively the meaning of marriage, know that their marriage is not a matter of the years but a deathless union invested with the radiance of eternal beauty and crowned with divine and perfect promise of immortal love.

Jewish teaching has always emphasized that even in marriage, each partner must fully respect the other partner's individuality. The Talmud states that a man should "love his wife as himself and honor her more than himself." A husband must never cause his wife to weep, Judaism says, for "God counts her tears." Husbands are taught: "Try to fulfill your wife's wishes, for it is the same as doing God's will." Everything can be substituted, Judaism says, "except the wife of one's youth." If a man's wife dies during his lifetime, we are advised, it is as though the world falls into darkness, and the husband's wisdom diminishes; it is as though he witnessed the destruction of the Holy Temple. And the Talmud teaches: "A husband's death is felt by none than the wife; a wife's death by none but her husband."

In Judaism, marriage, in the words of Eugene Mihaly, "is a voluntary union of two equals who find completion and wholesome fulfillment in each other...Judaism teaches that marriage can take place only by mutual consent."

In ancient times, when child marriage was a common practice, the rabbis taught that a father was forbidden to "betroth his minor daughter until she attains her majority, and declares 'I love this man.'" And following the formal wedding ceremony, a groom was not permitted to enter the nuptial chamber, without the bride's permission. The great scholar and rabbi, Maimonides, more than a millennium ago, taught that bride and groom were not allowed to "have sexual intercourse while either is drunk, or sluggish, or in mourning, nor when the woman is asleep, nor by overpowering her, but only with the consent and happy mood of both."

As Mihaly explains it:

> The sexual act of marriage is not something hidden, or obscene, or under a shadow of sin or shame, but a desired end in itself—the culmination of a loving relationship in which both partners have an equal share and find mutual satisfaction. The sex act is not condoned or given legitimacy by the necessity to propagate the race. On the contrary: the beauty, the character, the health of the offspring is influenced by the nature of the sexual relations. As the Talmud says: "He who coerces his wife will produce unworthy children."

If a husband is planning to divorce his wife, he should not have sexual relations with her. And when a wife is with her husband and thinks of another man during the sex act, that is forbidden and is regarded as adultery. Indeed, anticipating all the modern sexology books, the rabbis of old taught, before the sex act, the married couple should indulge in some play and become psychologically ready for the sexual act. The rabbis even taught that a husband who shows concern for his wife's sexual needs will be awarded sons and beautiful children. All forms of sexual play are permitted in Judaism, so long as both partners seek to fulfill their natural desires. Rabbi Meir, in the Talmud, declares that ideally the sex act should be as fresh and satisfying as on the couple's wedding night; care should be taken, he adds, that the act should not be perfunctory and routine. In the thirteenth century, a distinguished rabbi warned women who allowed their appearance to deteriorate "that a curse should descend upon them if a woman who has a husband does not try to be attractive."

Scholars of Judaism, throughout the centuries almost,

have noted that the rabbis who amended and adjusted the biblical laws always strove to fashion one single standard for husband and wife, one in which the wife would be regarded as a full and equal partner in the marital relationship. It was this single focus that gradually eliminated the ancient practice of polygamy, equalized the husband's duties with the wife in the responsibilities of marriage, and made divorce for a woman (and the disposition of property rights) more equitable and just than they had been at the dawn of Jewish history.

Many commentators have noted that the biblical tale of Adam and Eve really set the standard for the husband-wife relationship. First, we see that marriage is established for one man and one woman. Second, we note that Eve has a mind of her own, even if it leads to eventual expulsion from the Garden of Eden. Third, her husband stands by her, notwithstanding her succumbing to the snake's blandishments. Fourth, they bond together when tragedy strikes their son Abel.

The importance of early monogamy in Jewish practice cannot be overemphasized. Polygamy was virtually unknown for many centuries, and the tenth century ban issued by Rabbi Gershom seems to have been merely a legal, formal declaration outlawing this ancient practice. Indeed, historians maintain that although there was polygamy to some extent among Jews up to the tenth century, it was tolerated reluctantly in Jewish teaching. As the historian Israel Abraham has written: "It was the relapse into polygamy which Judaism owed to foreign influences, while its acceptance of monogamy had been an original, not an acquired, virtue."

According to Halachah, Jewish religious law states that while a husband is required to provide for his wife, he also has a claim on her earnings. But, if the wife so wishes, she may claim the right of self-support, and may keep her earnings. Her husband however may not make a similar claim—he is, under all circumstances, required to provide for her. Further, the husband may not sell his wife's property, or mortgage it; if he does, the law states that those transactions are null and void. Some talmudic authorities, wishing to protect the wife who perhaps was not as skilled in business affairs as was the husband, forbade her from transferring to him—by sale or outright gift—any of her property. The husband, however, was permitted to transfer his property to her.

As is well-known, the husband is required to provide his wife with food, clothing, shelter and the satisfaction of her conjugal needs. Furthermore, the talmudic rabbis expounded, he was required to furnish her with suitable ornaments and pocket money. The rule, the rabbis taught, was that "the wife ascends with her husband but does not descend with him." She is thus entitled to enjoy her married status, and at the same time she was not allowed to reduce her status, which she enjoyed when she lived in her parents' home. If a husband abandons his wife, Jewish law stipulates, the communal court has the right to grant her alimony from the husband's property; what's more, in order to spare her the embarrassment of appearing before the court as a mendicant, the court could make arrangements whereby a monthly sum of funds for sustenance purposes would be delivered to her.

If husband or wife maintain that visits by their respective parents, or other relatives, result in unpleasantness, either one could insist that such visits be discontinued. However, both the husband and the wife have every right to visit their families, without the spouse, whenever they wish.

If the husband decides that he wishes to change his vocation, or he wishes his family to move to a new residence, his wife must be in full agreement. He cannot force his wife to accompany him to a far off city and claim that this will be the new domicile of the family. Jewish law states that such behavior could be grounds for a divorce action brought by the wife.

Indeed, if a wife—after a reasonable amount of time of married life—decides that her husband married her under false pretenses, or that he is immoral, or that his source of livelihood is unacceptable to her, or if they are sexually incompatible, she may appeal to the religious court for a divorce. Other reasons that the court recognizes that are grounds for the wife suing for divorce include—if he embarrasses her, if he prevents her from entering their home, if he makes demands on her that would cast a pall on her reputation, if he is quick to lose his temper, if he insults her, or beats her, or leaves her for an unreasonable period of time.

Obviously if a wife learns, or actually sees, that her husband is having an affair with another woman, such an act would certainly fall under being an insult to her, or her being publicly humiliated and embarrassed.

On the other hand, a husband could sue for divorce on the basis of many reasons. For example, according to the esteemed Rabbi Akiva, if "another woman appeared more attractive to him." This certainly sounds like an extremely liberal divorce law, but historians are quick to point out that the dissolution of a marriage on such grounds, or for other reasons, was relatively rare in the Jewish community, right through the ages. A talmudic note says that "the altar sheds tears over him who divorces his first wife... the Lord hates sending away" the innocent wife. This seemed to be the prevalent attitude.

If Judaism is anything, it is direct and realistic. There is a common belief in the Jewish tradition that if a marriage is devoid of love, or caring, of mutual compassion—all of which lead to sanctity in marriage—it is best to dissolve the marital bonds and permit the two people the freedom to try again with another. As Eugene Mihaly says, "To punish the partners in an impossible marriage, and to deny them the opportunity for fulfillment with more suitable mates, would be inconceivable within Judaism."

Abraham A. Neuman was a specialist in Jewish life in the Middle Ages. He wrote: "The medieval Jewish communities could rightly boast of standards so superior to those of their environment as to defy their adversaries with the challenge that the truth of a religion is proved by the morality of its adherents."

When you consider that assessment, and then fast forward to our own day, you realize how accurate that evaluation really is. In another way of putting it: So long as the Jews lived a life that could really be described as Jewish, with its emphasis on ethics and morality, then their chances for a happy life, and of course a happy marriage, were enhanced. But when they moved away from Judaism's heritage and teachings, the odds of a happy, fulfilled marriage changed—they decreased.

That of course is a very broad generalization, and many readers might very well disagree. Certainly, there are many exceptions, both pro and con this belief. But, the authors of this book, a happily married couple for more than fifty years, have learned a thing or two. And they found that adhering to the traditions of Judaism, continually enlarging their knowledge of the classic Jewish texts, renewing—as it were—their spiritual batteries on Shabbat and holidays...somehow, it all works.

Nowadays, the divorce rate among Jewish couples is reaching the same high numbers that already exists in the general community. Divorce is not like buying a new car every year or two, to keep up with the latest models. It is a wrenching, destructive process that affects not just the two people involved but also the children, presuming there are any, and the families and friends on both sides. The ideal of marriage as being a sacred state entered into by two people voluntarily can and should be idyllic.

In the Middle Ages, the past two or three centuries, and to a lesser extent in the final years of the twentieth century, Jews were often singled out for their stable marriages and their high moral standards. Family and individual morality always have been, in Judaism, sacred tenets. If a husband was deemed unfaithful, and he was a member of the Jewish community, he was denounced openly. If a wife was even suspected of infidelity, a suspicion in which the husband joined—this was considered calamitous. In medieval days, the Jewish court would forcibly separate the two spouses, even against the husband's will. Holy matrimony was regarded as something the whole community had a part in, and infidelity was seen as a deliberate desecration of God's name. It was a deliberate transgression against God, and the community—in past centuries more so than today—saw such behavior as a profanation of God. Looking the other way was simply not considered a viable option.

Sometimes, in the Middle Ages, this attitude could also be cruelly mishandled. For example, if a bride was rumored to have had a previous betrothal agreement, the rumor had to be dispelled before the planned wedding. On the Sabbath before the wedding ceremony, when the synagogue was filled with worshipers, the local rabbi would stand up and announce the existence of a rumor, and demand that if anyone present knew anything pertinent, they were to appear before the court before the wedding as witnesses. If anyone knew anything and declined to testify, that person could be excommunicated from the Jewish community.

If no negative information was forthcoming, then the rabbi would permit the wedding to take place, and issue orders that the reputation of the bride and her family was subsequently not to be sullied.

If a husband heard rumors of infidelity about his wife, and he chose not to believe them, then the rabbinical court could allow them to live together as man and wife. This would hold true even if there was a witness who saw the wife commit acts of unfaithfulness. But, if there were two such witnesses who swore upon oath that they had seen an act of infidelity, then the husband could be compelled to accept the court's decree of separation of husband and wife.

In this day and age, most people would regard such a decree as harsh. Many couples, we may be certain, experience crises similar to events that took place in the Middle Ages, but they have learned to "forgive and forget." In the Middle Ages, the rules were more strictly enforced; marriage was looked upon as a sacred bond in which God Almighty had a hand, and therefore any act of infidelity was viewed as a sin against Him.

As Neuman writes of life in the Middle Ages: "Once the sacredness of the marriage tie was violated, it was declared irrevocably broken, and no course was left to the unhappy family but to resign themselves to the grim consequences. The blow to the family often struck innocent members as well as the guilty and, at such times, the rabbis were reluctant to pronounce the harsh decree. As far as was consistent with truth and their sacred responsibility, they strained every effort to vindicate the innocence of the accused persons or to resolve favorably any doubt. Thoroughly humane was the special considerateness shown by the rabbis to the accused woman if she was a mother."

CHAPTER SEVENTEEN

When a Man Or a Woman Is Incomplete

The *Midrash* teaches that a man without a wife, a woman without a husband, the two together without the Divine Presence—such people are incomplete, not fully fashioned, and incapable of living a full, satisfying life. Without marriage, and all the blessings that a good marital union brings, a person merely exists. Where there is love, understanding, mutual respect, intellectual and spiritual growth, dependable companionship—then it can be said that a person is fully alive, and enjoying his or her life deeply and truly.

Many a thoughtful analyst claims that in the final years of the twentieth century, most people have grown more selfish and greedy. On the other hand, there are those who disagree and insist that the world has always been the way it is now, but the superior communications we have makes it possible for everyone to know virtually everything in record time; hence, these charges of a crueler, greedier world.

With rare exceptions, there is little doubt that the world is a hard, harsh place, and that the number of people who can honestly be described as selfless and kindly seems to be shrinking every year. Are the traits that we recognize in the people around us, therefore, the same old ones that existed thousands of years ago, or are we in an age of frightening misanthropy? It is difficult to offer an accurate reply. The voluntary charitable contributions of millions of people to support the sick, the needy, the helpless and hopeless continue to remain very high, and even inspiring; and yet, abject poverty surrounds us—the disconcerting and depressing views of homeless families living on the streets of urban centers with little prospects of shelter for them in the offing.

We look to our political leaders for promises to end people's misery, and inevitably the solutions to these problems turn out to be fraudulent. In such a world, fortunate people—married people whose love for their spouses continues to expand—realize how lucky they are. Spouses, in a happy marriage, are the best of friends. Their friendship for each other is both supportive and strengthening.

In a good marriage, a husband confides in his wife all of his fears, anxieties, and his plans for the future. The same, of course, holds true for a wife. Together, when there is a time of difficulty, or a real crisis, each partner can bolster the other—selflessly. The husband and wife thus share good times and bad, and their devotion to one another, and their esteem for each other, continues to grow through the years. Sometimes it seems that there is no more room for a true love to expand, but miraculously there is. After a given number of years the husband and wife have forged together a single entity which confronts the world with doubled strength—and all this at the same time that each marital partner continues to maintain his or her individuality and uniqueness.

If one believes that the Torah, the Hebrew Bible, is a magnificent guidebook to life itself, then one need merely conduct one's married life according to its teachings. In the very first volume, Genesis, God declares that "it is not good that the man (Adam) should be alone; I will make him a helpmate against him." To which a sharp talmudic commentator said: "If he is worthy, she is a helpmate; if he is unworthy, she is against him."

The wise sages whose comments together formed the great tomes of the Talmud recognized the different motivations of men and women propelling them toward the wedding canopy. In the tractate of Yevamot, a rabbi said: "More than a man desires to marry, a woman desires to be married."

Choosing a wife is a challenging decision that usually comes along once in a lifetime. One must be wise in the selection, and lucky. Rabbi Akiva warned his disciples that "he who marries a woman he does not love violates five commandments of the Bible." Rabbi Barnett Brickner, in a comment he made in the 1940s, said that "success in marriage does not come merely through finding the right mate—but *being* the right mate." Jewish tradition has always emphasized that "man has free will in the choice of a proper wife."

Rabbi Meir, in the Talmud, declared that "marrying a daughter off to a boor is like throwing her to a lion." Rav, another talmudic sage, said "whoever marries for money will have unworthy children." In the *Book of the Pious*, published in Germany in the Middle Ages, Jewish youths on the verge of getting married were advised that "a young person need not obey his parents if they urge him to marry not the girl he loves, but another with money."

This same volume, a code of moral teachings, said that

it was better "to marry into a family of pure, kind and honorable proselytes rather than into a family of (born) Jews who lack these qualities." The Talmud advice however focuses on learning: "If necessary, sell all you have and marry the daughter of a scholar, and your daughter to a scholar." the Spanish Jewish philosopher of the Middle Ages, Joseph Zabara, cautioned prospective grooms not to "marry a woman for her money or beauty, for these vanish and the damage remains."

And yet, in spite of all the moral sagacious advice on getting married, and on creating a happy, fulfilling marital relationship, the great Yiddish author, Shalom Aleichem, best known for his *Fiddler on the Roof*, asked: "I ask you, my friend, who started all this business of marriage and of wives?" Some other Yiddish quips that describe marriage, presumably tongue in cheek:

> Even a bad match can produce good children.
>
> The man who marries for money—earns it.
>
> Husband and wife are one flesh, but have
> separate purses.
>
> The wedding ceremony lasts an hour but the
> troubles last a lifetime.
>
> There is no secret from one's wife.

For nearly a half-century, Jewish worshipers throughout the United States, Canada, Britain and other English-speaking countries have been studying the weekly biblical portion at synagogue services with the aid of Rabbi Joseph Hertz's remarkable commentary. Not as well-known but equally magnificent is Dr. Hertz's commentary on the prayer book. In the latter he spells out Judaism's approach to marriage:

> Marriage is that relationship between man and woman

under whose shadow alone there can be true reverence for the mystery, dignity, and sacredness of life. Scripture represents marriage not merely as a Mosaic ordinance but as part of the scheme of Creation, intended for all humanity.

They do less than justice to this divine institution who view it in no other light than as a civil contract. In a contract, the mutual rights and obligations are the result of agreement, and their selection and formulation may flow from the momentary whim of the parties. In the marriage relation, however, such rights and obligations are high above the fluctuating will of both husband and wife; they are determined and imposed by religion, as well as by civil law. The contract view fails to bring out this higher sphere of duty and conscience, which is of the very essence of marriage.

The purpose of marriage is twofold: (1) posterity (2) companionship.

(1) The duty of rearing a family figures in the rabbinic codes as the first of the 613 commandments of the Torah, 'Be fruitful and multiply.' To this commandment is due the sacredness and centrality of the child in Judaism. Little children are the 'Messiahs of mankind'—and the perennial regenerative force of humanity.

(2) Companionship is the other primary end of the marriage institution. Woman is to be the helpmate of man. A wife is a man's other self, and all that man's nature call for physical completion, as well as for social and spiritual wholeness. Only in marriage can man's need for physical and social companionship be directed to holy ends. This idea is expressed in the term *kiddushin*—Jewish marriage...a term that can best be explained as meaning the hallowing of two human beings to life's holiest goals. In married life, man finds his truest and most lasting happiness; and only through

marriage does human personality attain its highest fulfillment.

It is astonishing to note the amount of hostile misrepresentation that exists in regard to woman's position in Jewish life. Yet the teaching of Scripture is quite clear: 'God created man in His own image—male and female He created them.' Both men and women are akin to God in their spiritual nature, and are both invested with the same authority to subdue the earth and have dominance over it....A conclusive proof of woman's dominating role in Jewish life is the undeniable fact that the hallowing of the Jewish home was her work; and that the laws of chastity were observed in that home, both by men and women, with a scrupulousness that has hardly been equalled. The Jewish sages duly recognized her wonderful spiritual influence, and nothing could surpass the delicacy with which respect for her is inculcated.

There are some people, unfortunately lacking in knowledge of Jewish values, who claim that in Judaism there is no such thing as romantic love; further, they say, in the Jewish way of looking at things, marriage is a serious, almost business-like arrangement often supported by the parents of the bride and groom. These people are spouting ignorance! It is true that Jewish tradition regards marriage as far more than sexual mating; it is a new chapter in life designed to make two people more happy then they had been, affording them an outlet for their physical satisfaction, an opportunity to have and raise children and thus build a true family, and finally to develop with the marital partner a lifelong companionship that will grow ever stronger and fulfilling. Romantic love—within religious, traditional parameters—plays a very important part in choosing a marriage partner.

It is true that for many centuries prior to our own day

most marriages were arranged by the young couple's parents, who used as their criteria knowledge of the families involved, the degree of the young couple's learning, and their observance of Jewish religious law. It is also true that at times the bride and the groom hardly knew each other before the wedding. But what many critics of this traditional system fail to realize is that in the overwhelming majority of the cases, true love evolved—slowly but firmly—after the wedding and never ceased. In other words, married life itself brought in its wake a sense of love that neither partner could have foreseen as they stood under the wedding canopy. This does not mean that we are advocating returning to the arranged marriage system necessarily, although in many cases it probably is a good idea. But the young man or woman who brings home a potential spouse to introduce to the family may already have learned that the person they are in love with is an individual of learning, good deeds, considerateness, and shares many or most of the qualities of the potential partner.

How can anyone seriously claim that Judaism scoffs at romantic love? In his own way, Abraham loved Sarah deeply, as did Isaac love Rebecca. And what about Jacob who labored fourteen years to marry his true love, Rachel?

The *Song of Songs* is one of literature's most beautiful volumes of love poetry, and it is just as powerful today as when first composed. Judaism assumes that a husband will love his wife, and ergo there is no need to remind him to do so. However, there is a need to remind him to love God, and to love his neighbor, and to love the stranger. *Halachah*, Jewish religious law, goes so far as to say that if a man loves a woman, and his parents object to the match, and if the young lady is suitable and deserving, the young man should reject his parents' objections and marry her.

This, despite Jewish teaching that we must honor our parents.

*   *   *

One of the most touching of wedding customs, which follows immediately after the groom smashes the traditional glass (a reminder of the destruction of the Holy Temple in Jerusalem, and the couple is now legally and formally married) is *yichud*. A simple translation of this Hebrew word would be togetherness. After completion of the wedding ceremony, the newly-married couple seems to disappear. Guests, including the couple's parents and siblings, busy themselves generally checking on arrangements for dinner, talking to the photographer, the caterer and perhaps some friends and relatives they haven't seen for a long time. But where are the bride and groom?

Unobtrusively and speedily, they are whisked away to a small room to be alone for the first time as a married couple. Usually, the caterer has prepared a small snack for them, and they spend perhaps fifteen minutes in total privacy. The concept of now being husband and wife can be so overwhelming that the ancient rabbis who instituted this practice felt it was important for the two newlyweds to be alone for a short time to accustom themselves to their new status in life. Chances are the new couple, during this brief interlude of *yichud*, exchange words of love and admiration, hold hands, and allow the excitement of standing under the wedding canopy to wear off—so that they can begin their new roles calmly and without undue pressure.

After this brief togetherness, in most cases, the couple will emerge and rejoin their guests. There may very well be a formal receiving line in which the newlyweds, and their parents, greet friends and family before the formal dinner reception begins.

Traditionally, a newly married couple remains a bride and groom for a full year after the wedding. Indeed, in ancient times a groom was instructed to remain at home for a whole year after the wedding and acclimate his wife to her new status in life. If there was a war, in ancient Israel, he was excused from serving for the first year of his marriage. In modern Israel, however, this ancient ordinance has been brushed aside. Otherwise, possibly, there might be a sudden spate of weddings, with large numbers of Israeli soldiers asking for deferment because they had just been married.

*   *   *

In her delightful book, *The New Jewish Wedding*, Anita Diamant describes her search for a meaningful marital ceremony. Shunting aside two Jewish wedding extremes that were viewed by vast numbers of people on the movie screen—the film, *Goodbye, Columbus* and the film version of the hugely successful stage show, *Fiddler on the Roof*— the author says: "Since the 1970s countless (Jewish) couples have been married in ceremonies resembling neither *Columbus* nor *Fiddler*." Explaining why she sought to revive wedding customs abandoned by parents and grandparents, she said that she was not seeking a return to Orthodoxy nor an exercise in nostalgia, but "an evolving and dynamic synthesis of modern sensibilities and Jewish tradition." Noting that many, if not most, modern brides and grooms live together before marriage, and "fundamental expectations about marriage have changed in response to the changing status and self-consciousness of women, both in secular culture and within the Jewish community many of whom later convert to Judaism..."

The author also said that "Jews fall in love with and marry non-Jews in greater numbers than ever before." She sought to use her own forthcoming wedding as a model for modern young Jewish couples.

For example, she explained, using the nearly 2,000-year-old *ketubah*—the marriage contract—she and her husband-to-be amended the custom: it was read aloud during the ceremony, not in ancient Aramaic, but in English and modern Hebrew. And instead of being escorted down the aisle to the wedding canopy by parents, the couple chose to walk together. After the ceremony, the author added, when she and her new husband were brought to a small, private room for their brief interlude of aloneness, "it was a magical relief, a moment of truth, an island of peace in a gloriously hectic day."

* * *

The late Professor F. Alexander Magoun, who devoted many years to marriage counseling and the study of the phenomenon known as "love," said that he had—after considerable cogitation—arrived at a definition of the word that so often defies definition.

> Love, is a feeling of tenderness and devotion toward someone, so profound that to share that individual's joys, anticipations, sorrows and pain is the very essence of living. Love is the passionate and abiding desire on the part of two people to produce together the conditions under which each can be and spontaneously express his real self; to produce together an intellectual soil and an emotional climate in which each can flourish, far superior to what either could achieve alone.

In a happy marriage, the passage of time brings a couple closer—indeed, they grow together, spiritually, intellectually, emotionally. At any given time, husband or wife can practically know in advance what the other will say, or how they will react to a given problem. In Jewish mysticism there is a belief that each destined couple—before birth—separates into male and female individuals, and if they are lucky, they meet, come together, marry, and live happily after. So why should it be odd that they can, after a time, sense each other's thoughts and feelings?

In the words of the late Rabbi Ronald Gittlesohn, a heroic chaplain who served with the Marine Corps in the Pacific in World War II:

> Marriage is not a picnic. It does however have its experiences of indescribable happiness. These are enjoyed doubly under the impact of love.... The excitement and beauty of life are more than doubled when husband and wife share them in love. The tragedy and tribulation of life become ever so much easier to endure when love makes it possible for one to strengthen the other.

A half-century ago the Yiddish language was spoken, read and written by as many as ten million Jews. Since the Holocaust, and the passage of time, there has been the gradual decline of this wonderfully expressive language; Yiddish is not used as frequently as it deserves. In the Yiddish language there is one word that describes a perfectly matched couple—*zivig*. Actually, it is derived from a Hebrew term, meaning that a couple is matched up in heaven. Thus, if you are about to marry, and someone whose opinion you respect says that the two of you are a beautiful *zivig*—you must know that you've chosen the right lifetime partner.

CHAPTER EIGHTEEN

The Provocative Age in Which We Live

In his outstanding book, *The Jewish Way in Love and Marriage*, Rabbi Maurice Lamm approaches the difficult problem of sex, as practiced and looked upon by ultra-modern people in the waning years of the twentieth century. "Sex," Rabbi Lamm says unequivocally:

> ...is the most powerful, all-pervasive force in human experience. It may be intensely personal, meaningful and creative at one moment—and depersonalized, meaningless, and careless the next. Much of its glory is that it can bring us as close as we can get in life to experiencing the mystery of our mortality, and because of this it is sanctified. Yet, it can also be a blind, almost irresistible force seeking wanton release on the biological level, and in this way the sanctity is perverted.
>
> Paradoxically, sex—the most chaotic, powerful and untutored drive—can only be fully experienced when it includes an element of discipline and precision.

Citing an ancient comment in the Talmud, Rabbi Lamm quotes the sages as having said that "the greater the man, the greater the desire," thus putting both personal and sexual power on an equal level.

On all sides, from morning until night, we are surrounded by sexual temptations and influences. Think of what a day's ordinary contact stresses: sexually explicit photographs and artwork in advertising that seems to envelop all of us, all the time; think of the full color illustrations theoretically for the sale of clothing that seem to leap out at us from newspapers, magazines, wall posters, television images; think of attractive young women dressed with deliberate immodesty in mind. The overwhelming majority of movies and stage shows, not to mention music concerts, seem to be challenges to our morality. Where it will all end, no one seems ready to even hazard a guess.

Jewish teachings seem to be anachronistic in this day and age. On the surface, vast numbers of people seem to ridicule the very idea of sexual morality; not so very long ago—perhaps forty years—a couple contemplating marriage thought to "save" themselves for the bridal bed; at least the bride insisted on that prerogative. How different things are today! People who maintain family purity are scoffed at; young men and young women think nothing of having sex with someone they met a few hours earlier. The goal seems to be instant gratification. Just be careful, parents advise their children, conceding that their chances of teaching their children a more modest way of life are nonexistent.

Everything goes has become a universal motto. No pleasures are to be denied. This rush to enjoy immediate physical pleasure can be explained by some people as reflecting a generation's view that in the age of nuclear weaponry, people might as well enjoy themselves to the fullest extent possible. Who, after all, knows what the morrow will bring? When a young person is confronted by a parent, or an older sibling, and asked why this mad rush to "pleasure," including adulterous affairs and casual sex, the response usually is, "Well, it makes me happy!"

How empty the lives of such people must be. How shallow and how sad! Is there any wonder that the divorce rate continues to mount, and has already gone beyond fifty percent? Does it surprise us that the waiting rooms of mental health specialists—psychiatrists and psychologists—are filled with anxious, confused, misled patients?

Judaism through the ages has always regarded married sex as a beautiful source of mutual joy and pleasure, second only to the main purpose of married sex, namely, the creation of children who would carry on the family's history and destiny.

Probably there are very few Jews who have not seen Spielberg's great film, *Schindler's List*. More than one thousand Jews were saved from certain massacre by Schindler; when World War II ended, these Jews scattered around the world—to Israel, the United States, and various western countries. A half-century later, the film notes, those one thousand rescued Jews had married and raised families, and in the early 1990s numbered six thousand people.

In the Holocaust, where six million European Jews were deliberately massacred by the abomination known as Nazism, one and a half-million of those six million were children. What if they had been saved, somehow? Would they, forty or fifty years later, have numbered some eight or nine million Jews?

How then can young Jews planning to marry, in the final years of the horrific, bloody twentieth century, ignore their history and ignore the Bible's primary command: "Be fruitful and multiply"? Young Jewish families who put off having and raising children because both parents have to work to make ends meet, or because both parents want to fulfill themselves in their respective vocations, or because they don't want to bring children into a world of evil— these people need to look themselves in the mirror honestly and determine what is really important, and what is trivial.

Young parents who choose to go through life without children have made a decision that eventually leads to despair and emptiness. Children in the family are not only a whole new dimension for the parents, and of course the grandparents, but who is to say that such children will not one day find a cure for cancer, or compose a song that will fill the world with joy, or help connect us to a distant planet populated by people like us?

Sex in Jewish tradition is a vital component; it is not merely a source of "fun." Judaism teaches that sexual relations may take place between a man and a woman. Relations with an animal are regarded as perverse, and relations between members of the same sex are not allowed.

Sexual relations and marriage, Judaism teaches, are not permitted between a Jew and a non-Jew, nor of course between a Jew and a close relative, as listed in the Bible. Further, Jewish tradition says, sexual relations are a *mitzvah*, a religious command, when conducted within a hallowed marital union. Premarital sex is forbidden, and extramarital relations are basically crimes. Within marriage, Judaism teaches, sexual relations must be carried out in accordance with the laws of biblical purity (referring to a wife's menstrual cycle).

The talmudic sages devoted many years of study to advancing ideas that would lead to genuine family happiness and fulfillment. The talmudic tomes are replete with commentaries and arguments, covering every facet of family life. Studying these volumes today one quickly realizes how true is the biblical aphorism that "there is nothing new under the sun." We may fly across the ocean in a matter of hours, but the human soul is virtually the same as millennia ago—seeking real happiness, and fulfillment, and searching out why we are on this planet and how we must conduct ourselves during the short span of time that most of us reside on earth.

Rabbi Lamm has divided much of talmudic wisdom, in the area of sexual behavior, into seven basic conclusions:

(1) Human beings are not animals.

(2) Humans are not angels.

(3) Human sexuality is neutral and clean.

(4) A person's sexuality cannot be separated from that person's character.

(5) Only in the context of a genuine relationship does human sexuality have real meaning.

(6) Only in a permanent relationship does sexuality have value.

(7) Sexuality, to be meaningful, must be sanctified.

Each of the aforementioned axioms deserves to be considered and applied in one's life. "We are not animals"—one of the basic tenets of Judaism is that we are not animals, we are human beings created in the image of God. At the wedding service, one of the benedictions reminds the newlyweds that we are all made in God's image, and that we should not squander that very special distinction. In other words we cannot go through life simply obeying our instincts and ignoring the consequences. Such behavior leads to broken homes, loveless marriages, loneliness, unhappy spouses and children.

Although the sexual act between a human male and female may at first appear to be identical to that of an animal, it is not. The main difference lies in the fact that when two human beings engage in the act of physical loving, they both share in the action and in the caring for the other partner. It is not an act of selfishness, but rather an act of giving as well as taking. One of the eternal goals of Judaism is the hallowing and humanizing of all our drives; those who oppose Jews and Jewish teaching generally wish to secularize and even animalize Judaism's teachings.

Realistically, Jewish tradition says, although we are not animals, neither are we angels. In other words, we wish to uphold the highest possible moral codes promulgated in our faith, but we must acknowledge that we are not angelic. We do have sexual drives and we must learn to channel them, in marriage, in a desired direction. One of the first things that Judaism teaches is that we cannot go through life as celibates; after all, if we do not populate the world, who will? Judaism sees celibacy as an unnatural way of life completely at odds with Jewish traditions. We want to have children and raise them in the finest traditions that we can impart to them. That, we regard as a noble goal.

Judaism looks upon sex as a gift from God, with twin purposes: the propagation of the human species, and an instrument whereby married people can pleasurably grow even closer to one another.

In Judaism the sexual instinct is looked upon as neutral in the sense that by itself it is not bad, but how it is used determines what becomes of it. People are said to be born with two diametrically opposite instincts—the *yetzer tov* (the good inclination), and the *yetzer ra* (the evil inclination). The rabbis argue that even the so-called evil inclination cannot be dismissed out of hand: "Without the evil inclination, no man would build a house, get married, beget children, or pursue a livelihood." Sex, in other words, is not in itself bad; the abuse of sex is.

It does not require a rocket scientist to ascertain that our sexual lives are akin to our characters. Sexual love in a good marriage can be a very gratifying, joyous experience, no matter how often the couple indulges. But if one of the partners is mean-spirited, selfish and uncaring, chances are that that individual will turn the sex act into one where gratification and release are directed at himself or herself, with absolutely no concern for the needs or feelings of the other—in the same manner that such a person, caught in a desperate situation together with a number of other survivors of a plane crash, for example, would seek to save only himself. A person who lives by the philosophy of numero uno is not going to change when he enters the marital bed.

Scholars of the Holocaust have noted that there were two kinds of people who emerged from the Nazi concentration camp hellholes. Some came out cursing God and man, determined to bolster their material well-being, convinced that to survive in this cruel world one must be self-centered, cynical and brutally mean. The other survivors emerged from the Nazi hells determined to live as ethically and kindly as they possibly could, convinced that this was the only way humanity would survive, and seeking some kind of spiritual rationale for their horrible experience. While the inmates were locked up in Nazi camps, there were reports of some fathers tearing a piece of bread out of a child's hand so they could supplement their own meager ration; there were also reports of some fathers foregoing their own piece of bread and saving it for their child.

Fast forward these heart-wrenching reports to our own day: Imagine the same type of people getting married, and imagine—how will they act toward their spouses? Not only in the bedroom and during sexual relations but throughout the house and all week long. It is not hard to realize that character, a person's inner personality, will dominate the marriage, for better or worse.

A principal reason that Judaism condemns adultery, premarital sex, and casual sex is that these activities cannot possibly be relationships based on love and respect for one another, but rather—no matter how one wishes to designate them—wittingly or otherwise they turn into shoddy, depressing affairs.

Thus, inasmuch as sex is such a powerful human drive, it must be accompanied by deep, human, personal feelings—and not solely by purely biological motivations. Otherwise, we regress to the animal kingdom. In Jewish tradition, God—however we conceive Him—is above us all; just below Him are the angels, and below them are us, ordinary people, and below us, the animal kingdom. People, we are taught, should strive upwards, to reach higher than where we are, closer to the angels. If we do not strive to attain what is higher than us, then we may well slip down to the animal kingdom, below.

As one of the classic biblical commentators, Nahmanides, said about the rule in Genesis whereby we are instructed to leave our parents, wed and cleave unto our wife as one flesh: "First, one must cleave to his wife, then they will become one flesh. There can be no true oneness of the flesh without first experiencing a cleaving together of the heart."

One of the three things that a husband must provide his wife with is satisfaction of her sexual needs (plus of course food and clothing). The rabbis discussed this ruling, and agreed that the husband's readiness to fulfill his wife's conjugal needs must be accompanied by closeness and joy. Thus, the husband approaches his wife with all his heart and soul, and not merely to carry out a perfunctory physical act.

Human sexuality, Rabbi Lamm emphasized, has value

only in a permanent and recognized relationship. He writes: "For Judaism, value in human sexuality comes only when the relationship involves two people who have committed themselves to one another and have made that commitment in a binding covenant recognized by God and by society. The act of sexual union, the deepest personal statement that any human being can make, must be reserved for the moment of total oneness."

He stresses: "The sexual act is the first and most significant event of married life, and its force and beauty should not be compromised by sharing coitus in the expectation that some day a decision will be made to marry or not to marry. The act of sex is not only a declaration of present love, it is a covenantal statement of permanent commitment. It is only in this frame of reference that sexual congress is legitimate, because only then is it a religious act."

There is no single word in the Bible spelling out the equivalent of marriage. The great rabbinical commentators explain that the Hebrew word used today, *kiddushin*, which signifies both hallowing and betrothal, is followed by another Hebrew term, *nissu'in*, usually translated as nuptials and elevation. That is, the earlier state of sanctification is followed by the next stage of elevation, i.e., raising the sexual act to a higher, spiritual level. Perhaps that is why among Hasidim and also Orthodox Jews, conjugal relations are often planned for the eve of the Sabbath—Friday evening—when the aura of spirituality has descended on the home, and everything has already achieved a special ambience of joy and restfulness, all of which is followed by physical love.

CHAPTER NINETEEN

So, How Do You Choose the Right Partner?

Can anyone—parents, siblings, friends, relatives, anyone—advise and guide anyone on the selection of a marital partner? Jewish teaching carefully lists those marriages which are not permitted under Jewish law—intermarriage, incestuous marriage—and traditionally has gently suggested that a young person on the threshold of marriage should think carefully, look carefully, analyze with one's mind and not only one's heart the qualities of a prospective mate before taking the fateful step. After all, even if you devote many long years to studying a given profession, and you decide you really don't like the work, you can make a change. The same is true about renting an apartment or buying a house. But choosing a husband? A wife? It's supposed to be for a lifetime, under the best of circumstances.

So, how do you know if he or she is the right one?

We are reminded of a question posed to us by our younger grandson, at the time in his very early twenties and just out of undergraduate school. We knew he had been dating a particular young lady for some time, but he seemed unsure of his choice. Our grandson, on a plane heading to an island vacation, turned to us, his expression very serious:

"I want to ask you a serious question," he began. He took a deep breath. "How do you know if you've chosen the right person, you know, to marry, I mean."

Before my wife could respond, I leaned over and said: "You know, if you have to ask—she's not the right one."

He nodded and seemed to be lost in thought until we reached our destination.

*　　*　　*

There are a number of rabbinical and moralistic teachings in Judaism that obviously stress, both to the groom and the bride, the necessity to check into the families of the prospective mates, and always to seek out qualities of kindness, honesty, religiosity, and compassion. In the Bible's first volume, Genesis, we are told of Abraham's servant, Eliezer, who can perhaps be called the world's first matchmaker and who was charged by his master to find a suitable wife for his son, Isaac.

Eliezer had no precedents to fall back on and no criteria to choose from. Instead, wishing to carry out Abraham's instruction in the full spirit in which they were given to him, he prayed for divine guidance. It was not a formal prayer, but a "prayer of the heart." Abraham, in his great confidence in God's intervention in the matter, assured Eliezer that "He will send His angel before you, and you shall take a wife for my son from there." Abraham knew that God planned a very great future for the Jewish people, which made him absolutely certain that Isaac—the progenitor of the Jewish people—would wind up with a most suitable wife, and thus would help to fulfill God's promise to Abraham.

When Eliezer, after arriving at his destination, first sees Rebecca, the Torah tells us, he takes note of the fact that she is a beautiful woman and apparently also chaste; more importantly, however, she has an aura of generosity, hospitality to strangers, and kindness to the animal world. These fundamental traits have remained constant in describing a good Jew's character—and therefore, it is reasonable to conclude that in searching for a lifelong marital mate, we must look for people of the opposite sex who display these characteristics.

In Jewish tradition, compassion is one of three qualities regarded as fundamental to a good Jewish woman. The other two basic traits that women must exhibit are modesty and kindness. The *Shulchan Aruch*, the book of Jewish religious rules and regulations, stipulates quite plainly: "It is not right to marry someone who does not possess these characteristics... If someone is arrogant, cruel and hates people, and does no kindness it is suspected that" that person is not really Jewish. When scholars discuss a good marriage, or peace in the house, or good children—there is always some reference to at least one of these qualities.

Jews have always taken pride in being called *rachmanim b'nai rachmanim*. That is, they are compassionate people, the children of compassionate people. That does not mean that other peoples are not compassionate, but the degree of caring and kindness shown by Jewish communities in every section of the world, throughout history, cannot be compared. In the United States, for example, where the Jewish community in 1996 stood at about five and three-quarter million people, and perhaps somewhat less, they managed to raise extraordinary sums to provide food and shelter for co-religionists in lands of oppression and danger. That does not mean that Jews give only to Jewish causes, for they support a great range of deserving charities. A few years ago Jews—representing some two and a half percent of the American population—had raised the largest number of dollars for the United Jewish Appeal, while the rest of the country lagged behind in supporting various other charities.

The kindness that Rebecca showed to Eliezer's camels is said to be one of the early reasons why in Judaism the slaughter of animals for the purpose of eating must be done with a minimum of pain, and why a bird's eggs may not be taken from the nest while the mother bird is present, why an ox may not be muzzled while engaged in plowing, and why hunting as a sport is regarded (in Orthodox tradition) as a religious crime. Indeed, although it is customary to offer a blessing when donning a new garment, no blessing is pronounced over shoes—because the leather for the shoes meant that an animal had to be killed.

In our own day, when camels do not abound in downtown locations, we can determine if people are compassionate if they care about and help the widows, orphans, homeless, strangers, and the sick. Indeed, visiting the sick—known as the *mitzvah* of *bikur cholim*—is a very special sign that the person involved really cares; it is much easier to send off a check, but to go into the sickroom, and try to cheer up someone in need of encouragement takes an extra little something. The same of course can be said about the commandment of visiting the bereaved.

Modesty in Judaism is known as *ts'ni'ut*. It is important to be observed not only by women but by men too. The importance of modesty signifies that sexual relations are meant to be carried out in private, away from prying eyes. And both men and women, in order to keep morality at a high level, should not parade around in provocative, flashy clothes, but reserve such displays for their own mates, in private. In a traditional Jewish wedding, shortly before the bride and groom and their special, invited guests stand under the wedding canopy, awaiting the rabbi's officiating at the marriage ceremony, there is a small rite in which the groom covers the face of his bride with a veil of modesty. This is known as the *badeken* ceremony, and reminds us of Rebecca's reaction to Abraham's servant, Eliezer, bringing her to meet her future husband, Isaac. As soon as she saw her future spouse, Rebecca veiled her face, so that she would be regarded from that moment on as a married woman. This was a quintessential act of modesty, for she was no longer a woman alone in the world—but a consecrated woman, part and parcel of a man with whom she would very soon form a holy marital relationship.

The antonym for the term *ts'ni'ut* in Jewish thinking would be blatant immorality, flaunting of one's sexuality, arrogant vulgarity. The Talmud teaches that a woman has been given a divine gift—the ability to reproduce another human being, and this great gift must be protected and safeguarded, for in truth the same gift is available to a pig wallowing in the mud.

Generally speaking, when contemplating marriage, and when considering a lifetime partner, one should bear in mind the fact that in Judaism, learning is seen as the quintessential goal—and, it is stressed, it is not to be left only to scholars. Jews, both men and women, have always been encouraged to study the Torah, and to study it again and again, for each time one reads the famous and the not-so-famous biblical passages, a new insight emerges on how we must conduct ourselves on this planet, i.e., how we must behave toward God and how we must behave toward our fellow human beings.

These new insights and new understandings are meant to accompany us all through life. The older we get, the more we learn and understand, and the better we know how to cope with life's problems, both small and large. One of the complaints that a judge sitting in a domestic relations court often hears, whether from the husband or the wife, is that the other partner "did not grow along with me"—that is, did not develop more mature, more advanced ways of looking at changing circumstances in the couple's life.

But of course, to embark on a lifelong pursuit of learning and wisdom means that a person must possess a certain degree of intelligence; that is why the rabbis of old decreed that a "Torah scholar" who was the product of an illegitimate union "takes precedence" over a high priest who is an ignoramus. Thus, in the European *shtetl*, the Jewish hamlet, where material comforts were scarce but life was lived on a high spiritual level, parents would boast about their offspring by saying he or she was a *talmid chacham*, a true scholar. Most parents' goals in the period of a few hundred years ago could be summed up in the hope that their children would marry scholars, students, people with good minds and high spirits.

A famous Israeli rabbi on a visit to the United States, his first, tells of meeting many wealthy American Jewish businessmen, all of whom took him aside and confided that their fathers or grandfathers had been famous rabbis or scholars in the old days—not wealthy industrialists nor successful businessmen, but scholars, men of learning. That was their true claim to fame!

Throughout Jewish history, Jews have pursued Torah studies. Small boys (and later, girls too) were taught the alphabet from the age of three; by the age of six, the more gifted children could read and understand sections of the Talmud, which is written primarily in Hebrew and Aramaic—notwithstanding the fact that these students were largely brought up speaking the Yiddish language. Perhaps one of the reasons why Jews have won disproportionately large numbers of Nobel Prizes has been because of their innate love of learning.

So, Judaism says, marry a scholar's son or daughter. But, ask the rabbis of old, what if no such person is available? Then marry someone who is respected for his leadership in the community and for his charitable ways. If no such person was available, marry whoever keeps the communal charity fund; again, if he/she is not available, marry the offspring of the schoolteacher. The main thing to bear in mind was to avoid, at all costs, marriage to an ignoramus. In other words, choose an intelligent and intellectually gifted partner, when marrying, but even beyond that, the ancient rabbis cautioned, make sure your spouse will be one with whom you can live at home peacefully. Above all other goals, peace in the home—the ideal of *shalom bayit*—takes precedence.

Centuries ago, the sages-rabbis-talmudic commentators understood that a good person is not necessarily a good, observant Jew. One must observe all basic ethical tenets, but in addition a Jew should be God-fearing and eager to observe also Jewish religious rituals. The rationale here was that by observing the Sabbath and the Jewish holidays, a Jewish family would bring into their home a spirit of joy and conviviality, and that this in turn would bring about a year-round, ongoing ambience of celebration.

In this manner, a newly-married Jewish couple feel themselves quickly connected to the entire Jewish people, to Jewish history, to the Bible, and to a tradition that encompasses more than three and a half-thousand years of achievement. The new couple, by becoming quickly attached to the rhythms of Jewish life, senses that life is a great deal more than fancy furniture, vacation trips,

Broadway shows—but a whole cavalcade of ancient wisdom, and a whole array of great goals that must be attained, and by participating in all of these religious-educational-cultural-spiritual activities, one's heart and mind will be stretched and grow and reach new dimensions that will provide a deep sense of belonging.

Lest the reader misunderstand that this is a call for extremism in the religious life of a newlywed couple: Judaism's teachers through the ages have always advised that the Jewish religion, the Jewish way of life, should be explained gently, and that it should not seek to coerce the other into observance that is not accepted with love and understanding. In Judaism, the objective is to teach with kindness and patience, never with threats or fear. It is through the search for understanding of God, and the eventual love of God, that a marriage partner should decide to become a committed, practicing Jew.

In the Wall Street area, in recent years, there is a new, almost mind-boggling phenomenon: Brokers and people involved in the frantic life of the financial world bring their lunch to work one day of the week, and meet in the boardrooms of large, distinguished corporations. They nibble on their brown bag sandwiches while a young rabbi, usually, explains for two hours the meaning and moral teaching of a talmudic passage. The number of people involved in these classes is probably in the hundreds, but it is proof—if proof were needed—that a great many educated, youngish American Jews are searching for a deeper meaning of life, and of their Jewish roots, and of a way to bring more spiritual, intellectual and emotional meaning to their families, including themselves.

* * *

When trying to make up one's mind about a prospective

mate, one should look at the candidate and wonder: What kind of parent will this person be to our children? This is especially true of a wife, since traditionally the mother spends more time than the father in guiding a child's development. A prospective mate and a parent for prospective children must, of course, be an individual of integrity, honesty, and unquestioned honor. After all, children are easily swayed by what their parents do, as well as by what they say.

This is not as easy as it sounds. When a young person is "in love," unfortunately that individual does not always think clearly and soberly about the character traits of the potential partner. The truth is that in all too many cases, where the marriage did not work out, one or both of the prospective partners could not wait to go to bed with the other, and pushed aside all other doubts and questions.

Which of course is too bad, and helps to explain the high, and still growing, divorce rate. It's as though you were considering buying a new car, and all you saw were the trim lines, the flashy color, and the name on the hood—and you bought it without checking the engine, without asking the many questions that experienced car buyers always ask.

And that's only a car! This is marriage, we're talking about. The union of two people, for what is hoped will be a long lifetime of joy, comfort, children, and eventually grandchildren.

A young person in the early formative years is influenced by the family. That is clear and is not always appreciated fully. There is a wide degree of difference among talmudic scholars who believe that the boys and girls grow up taking after either the father or the mother. The great Maimonides believed that if a boy resembles his father, his years on earth will be like the father's; on the other hand, the Mishna taught that a father "endows his son with looks, strength, wealth, wisdom and longevity;" Rabbi Bahya insisted that "sons will follow, in their values, the maternal family, for such is the nature of wine—after a while it tends to take on the taste of the vat."

Some sages said the daughters resembled the mother and followed her life pattern, while others disagreed and said daughters followed in their fathers' footsteps. One ancient rabbinic aphorism claimed that the groom, before marriage, "should check out the wife's brothers, because his future sons would follow in the wife's brothers' footsteps."

Judaism teaches that before getting married we should shy away from children of immoral women. The greatly-admired French Jewish commentator, Rashi, said, on this issue: "See for yourself a quiet family. Generally, an argumentative family is not of authentic Jewish descent. Because of their spiritual defect, which they try to live down, they implant hatred in themselves and become quarrelsome. The legitimate Jewish families of Babylon are the quiet ones, because they are sure of their nobility."

There are of course many exceptions—there are plenty of cases of selfish parents whose children turn out to be outstanding people; and there are also cases of parents who by all standards are fine people, but whose children grow up as failures. There are no hard and fast rules but there are rules, where the majority of the time indicates that such and such will happen—but not always.

The greatly-admired Rabbi Raphael Samson Hirsch, a religious philosopher who lived in the nineteenth century, offered advice to a man about to choose a wife (adding that it also applied to a woman selecting a husband):

> When you choose a wife, remember that she is to be your companion in life, in building up your home, in the performance of your life task, and choose accordingly. It should not be wealth or physical beauty or brilliance of

mind that makes you decide whom to marry. Rather, look for richness of heart, beauty of character, and good sense and intelligence. If, in the end, you require money, and your wife's family freely offers it to you, you may take it, but woe to you and your future household if you are guided only by considerations of money.

Study well the character of your future wife, but since character is first revealed by contact with real life, and since the girl first comes into contact with real life only after marriage, look well at her family. If you see a family in which disputes and quarreling are rife, in which insolence and evil talk are common, in which you behold hard-heartedness, hate and uncharitableness, do not attach yourself to it.... Our sages recommend that one should always look for the daughter of a learned man, of a man in whom the public has shown its confidence by entrusting him with communal office; above all, of a man whose daughter can be expected to have learned practical wisdom from the example of her father.

CHAPTER TWENTY

The Apocrypha Taught: "A Good Wife Is a Gift"

The rabbis of ancient times were as understanding and insightful of man's needs, foibles and strengths as our wisest analysts of the modern era. In the Apocrypha, it is written that a "good wife is a gift to her husband... a beautiful wife has a fortunate husband, the days of his life are doubled... but turn away from a flirtatious woman, lest she catch you in her net."

A woman's beauty, the rabbis taught, was a positive, desirable feature, but it should not be a woman's preeminent trait. It may swiftly vanish, and then what remains? they asked.

Realistically, they also noted that wealth was desirable, and did not teach that poverty was character-building or noble. Poor people have to spend so much energy and time trying to make ends meet, they have little time for Torah study; the struggle to earn a livelihood warps the values, and the poor person is deprived of an opportunity to live on a higher plane, enjoying life's spiritual gifts. In our prayers we hope for an easy, decent income, so that we may have the time and strength to pursue religious study. On the other hand, money per se is not a crime—it is only when a person devotes excessive efforts to making money that his/her values becomes skewed and one loses his/her place on the true track of life. Perhaps that is why many people who pursue financial rewards first and foremost seek to compensate for their ways by providing generously for schools and other noteworthy cultural and religious causes.

In the *shtetl* days it was customary for wealthy in-laws to provide for a poor but gifted son-in-law, encouraging him to study during the first years of his marriage to their daughter. Indeed, it was regarded as a privilege to be able to support a young family in this manner. On the other hand, there were of course young husbands who demanded funds from their in-laws, sometimes claiming that they were scholars and thus deserving extensive financial support. These people, and others who sought to exploit fellow Jews for financial rewards, were sharply condemned by the rabbis.

It was customary, until very recently, for a bride's parents to present the groom with *nad'n*, a dowry, to help the new couple get started. At times, the bride's parents were short of funds, and at times the groom would back out of the wedding—causing his wife-to-be profound anguish. Anyone who knowingly causes such pain to his bride, the rabbis warned, "will have unworthy children, his marriage will be bad, he will never be prosperous." On the other hand, if the groom is understanding of the situation with respect to the lack of funds, he will be blessed and his marriage eventually will be most successful.

*   *   *

Before selecting a marital mate, the rabbis cautioned, one should be wary of the prospective partner's negative traits. The Talmud noted that two common characteristics one should look out for are the person who cannot compromise and always seeks out "perfection." Another characteristic to be aware of in a possible marriage partner, and to try hard to avoid, is the person who is constantly angry. Also, the rabbis warned, make every effort to stay away from people who are regularly bad-tempered and argumentative. Such people do not normally possess the components with which a happy, successful, fulfilling marriage is built.

Another negative trait to avoid, the rabbis warned, was found in a woman divorced for her immorality. A man who regards himself as ethical and moral may find being wed to such a woman too difficult. Although Jewish law permits such a union, the husband may never cease to worry that the moment he leaves home, his wife may revert to her old lifestyle. One talmudic dictum says one may marry the daughter of a woman of immoral reputation, but not the woman herself. Summing up, the Talmud advises a prospective marriage partner to marry someone who has a gentle temperament, is genuinely modest, and can be described as industrious.

The *Book of the Pious* states however that even if a bridegroom-to-be knows his future wife is modest, which many people regard as the noblest of traits, he should not marry her "if she is bad-tempered." Such a wife, the husband-to-be is cautioned, would in all likelihood disrupt the most important factor in a happy marriage, *shalom bayit*—a peaceful household.

* * *

Throughout history, marriage has been a powerful and

fundamental institution, alongside the concept of the family. Nonetheless, history records cyclical explosions of popular sentiment against marriage and against the idea of family.

Surrounded nowadays by surging outbreaks of crime and violence, threatened by nuclear disaster, fearful of an overpopulated world and of a planet that is warming constantly, with some Cassandras promising that the icy oceans of the North and South Poles will someday soon melt and engulf the world as we know it—men and women seem to be hell-bent on a course of self-destruction. Marriage and the family, to these people, are antiquated, outdated ways of life. They want to try everything but, it seems. How else do we explain bizarre clothing on young people, bizarre behavior in school and at home, heavy drinking, widespread use of addictive drugs that promise nirvana and deliver instead death and destruction? The phenomenon of urban homelessness coupled with hundreds of thousands of people—if not millions—living on the sidewalks and awaiting handouts has become commonplace. We are blasé about these horrors, although deep-down we are too horrified to confront them with a genuine program of action that might offer a solution to these problems.

Any wonder that growing numbers of young marrieds choose not to have children? Why bring children into such a cruel world? The late and lamented Rabbi Joseph B. Soloveitchik taught that the biblical phrase that preceded the emergence of Eve referred to Adam's loneliness, not to his being alone. Therefore, marriage was created as part of the divine plan, namely, birth, followed by marriage, and then inevitably death.

Those who claim the world is just too corrupt and evil for a new generation of children are in effect thwarting God's divine plan; what is more, they are depriving themselves of one of life's greatest, deepest, most meaningful sources of genuine joy and fulfillment.

True enough, in these final years of the twentieth century, the world is a mess. Crime and drugs and homelessness, and a general malaise, are worse than horrible—they cause every thinking person despair and anguish. But—in every generation of mankind, and certainly in every period of Jewish history, things have been awful. Bloodshed between tribes, cities, nations has never really ceased. Persecution, oppression, enslavement, exploitation—they have been with us for as long as we can remember.

For Jews, the horror of the Holocaust has never been surpassed. And yet, Judaism is a faith of hopefulness, and we go on, hoping for better times. And better times do come. Think of Israel: Three years after the end of World War II, when Jews in every part of the world believed they had reached the nadir of their history, Israel was reestablished—after nearly two thousand years of exile. The large Jewish community of the Soviet Union that had been ruthlessly separated from the world Jewish community has finally been permitted to leave that totalitarian dictatorship, and nearly one and a half-million Jews have resettled in Israel and the United States. And the Soviet Union itself has collapsed!

The survivors of the Holocaust, almost as soon as they were physically able, married and began having children. Think back to the Israelites' bondage in Egypt: What if the parents of Moses, a newborn Jewish male child, had obeyed the Pharoah's edict and put him to death at birth? We would not have had Moses, the great Lawgiver. If not Moses, who would have led the Israelite slaves out of Egypt to the Promised Land? If there had not been Moses, would God have given the Torah to another? Would the world perhaps not have had a Bible or would it have taken a few more millennia before another Moses arose?

In Judaism, the idea of getting married means completion. Both the bride and groom become complete human
beings when they unite in marriage. As the blessing
offered under the wedding canopy says, may this new
couple be as happy as the first human couple was in the
Garden of Eden. Marriage, in Jewish tradition, is a union
among three—the bride, the groom, and God. It is a divine
concept and action. Thus, if a partner in the marriage
misbehaves or is unfaithful, he or she sins not only against
the marital partner but against God Himself.

The idea of celibacy, in Judaism, is viewed as withdraw-
ing from real life, and ignoring a biblical command to have
children. Not only are there no celibate monks or nuns in
Judaism, but the whole idea is seen as a refutation of a
divine command. Just as every person in the Jewish
scheme of things can approach God directly, in prayer and
supplication, so must every Jewish man and woman seek
to propagate a new generation. To paraphrase Hillel, if not
us, then who?

*　*　*

Why do so many former Russian Jewish couples who
emigrate and resettle in the United States or Israel seek
out a rabbi and ask to be married again, only this time in
a Jewish religious ceremony? Perhaps the best explanation
lies in Rabbi Maurice Lamm's wonderful book, *The Jewish
Way in Love and Marriage*:

> Love seeks eternity, sanctity...true lovers cannot endure
> in a hastily-put-together arrangement. Love will not be
> fulfilled until it reaches that ultimate moment, the total
> commitment of marriage. Love is a sacred trust. The
> description of the relationship of bride and groom
> preserved in the blessing at the wedding service is *re'im
> ahuvim*—beloved friends. The secular sanction of a civil

marriage is not enough to motivate love to rise to its highest level; it needs the sanctification of an almighty and eternal God. Love so desanctified cannot long withstand the daily frustrations, angers and hurts. To flourish, love needs an intimation that it originates in the plan of the Creator; that the world could not exist without it; and that an all-knowing God delights in it.

* * *

Judaism cannot stress enough its deep commitment to the concept that in a truly good marriage both partners, although totally linked to each other, are at one and the same time separate, individual personalities. Their love for each other merges them, but they must never feel that they are submerged in the marriage. The philosopher Erich Fromm, writing of love, and citing its beauty and its paradox, said that "two beings become one, and yet they remain two."

Historians have commented on the fact that the story of the Jewish people, which stretches back some three and a half thousand years, is the story of a family. To this day we speak of Abraham, Isaac and Jacob as our forefathers, and of their wives Sarah, Rebecca, Leah and Rachel as our matriarchs, which is really another way of saying mothers. Non-Jewish theologians who have studied the Jewish people in an effort to determine what the Jews are—a religion, a race, a people—have concluded that the best way to allude to them is as the House of Israel, of *Bait Yisrael*. The Ethiopian Jewish community, cut off from the mainstream of world Jewry for more than two millennia, came to be called *Beta Yesrael*, the House of Israel. The prophets, referring to the special relationship that exists between God and the Jewish people, described it as husband (God) and wife (the Jews). Co-religionists are regarded as brothers, while the term *re'im* (neighbors) is reserved for non-Jews.

It hardly needs to be stressed that when a member of the Jewish community wins a Nobel Prize or does something that will be a boon to mankind, Jews generally feel family pride in the accomplishment. And, if on the other hand, a Jew is arrested for criminal activity, virtually every Jew feels a sense of shame—family shame.

Attempts were made in recent years to eliminate the traditional Jewish family concept, and with it the idea of a Jewish marriage. Marx espoused doing away with it, and the Soviets did away with it; it did not take long before they rescinded their decision and reintroduced a respectful attitude towards the family. Experience has shown that the family is the best and most dependable source of learning for young children—learning how to deal with people, how to become an ethical, honest person, how to bolster links to parents, siblings and other relatives. A good family home becomes for most people throughout their lives a source of stability. That is why the rabbis advised young husbands to call a wife "home," for she and the home always represented a sure source of morality, a true place of warmth and love.

Compare the Latin word with the Hebrew word for a womb. In Latin the word is *hysteria* while in Hebrew the term is *rechem*. The Latin term refers to the physical convulsion before birth. The Hebrew word is linked to the Hebrew word for compassion.

For mankind to continue on earth, people must have children, and raise them and educate them, and lead them on a moral path. Isaiah said simply "God created the world to be inhabited." And the talmudic commentators explained that "one who does not participate in the 'be fruitful and multiply' ruling causes God's presence to disappear... If there are no children after you, on whom will the Divine Presence dwell? On sticks and stones?"

There is a Hebrew word, *davka*, that is difficult to translate. The best way of explaining it is to say it means "just because." *Davka* because the Nazis sought to obliterate the Jews from the face of the world, we will not aid them in their diabolical scheme by refraining from having children. *Davka* because there is so much evil and peril in the world, we will have children and raise them, and hope they will turn into the kind of people who will lead the world to a happier, more positive path.

* * *

People living in the twentieth century find it hard to fathom how two individuals who have never spent any time together, who hardly knew each other, and who were extremely young could have married—and, to no one's special surprise, could have developed and maintained a happy, productive, and to all intents and purposes, successful marriage.

Matches in the Middle Ages were arranged by the fathers, and sometimes with the aid of professional matchmakers. Fathers who knew each other as a result of business contacts, or perhaps through being regular worshipers in the local synagogue, or maybe they were even distant cousins, felt a responsibility to match up their children as soon as they began to enter their middle or late teens. Generally the fathers sought, in arranging a match, a prospective marital partner who could be discerned as a person of integrity, with a penchant for learning, and possessing a healthy respect for parents and family. If, in addition, the young people could be said to be handsome or beautiful, and also people of means, so much the better. The main objective in making the arrangements was that the young person in question would enter the other's family and be regarded by all as a *mentsh*—a truly nice person, in every sense of the term.

There were times of course when matching up two people was not an easy matter. The young man or the young woman was the opposite of good looking; perhaps one or both of them limped, or was hard of hearing, or spoke with difficulty. Sometimes the fathers themselves were not especially outgoing and did no really know any suitable candidates. And then there were also occasions when the matter of a dowry stood in the way—there was not enough money to help a young couple get started on the path to marriage. Under these circumstances, the matchmaker—the *shadchan*—had a role to fill. For a fee he would try to put two people together, using his insights into human strengths and weaknesses, in which he had become an expert after bringing couples together for many years.

What people nowadays find so hard to understand is that despite the fact that the husband and wife really only met at their wedding—although they may have had merely a nodding knowledge of one another—they did not expect to fall in love, before the wedding ceremony. Their understanding was that after living together as man and wife for a given time, after having and raising children, after struggling to build a home and better their economic standing—then, and only then, would there grow between them a special mutual feeling that could be called love, and that seemed in the vast majority of cases to satisfy them.

The modern idea of falling in love, before the wedding of course, was as foreign and inconceivable as is the idea today of two people marrying because their fathers believed they would make a good pair. How things change! But—who can say that today's young couples flourish and grow into happy, fulfilled couples? How can we forget the fifty percent divorce rate? No one can say for sure that the Jewish couples of a few hundred years ago were happier than those of today, but chances are that they were. Their expectations may have been more modest; there may very well have been a great deal more children about who needed care and attention, and both parents were therefore too busy taking care of them to worry about being happy.

Until the ninth or tenth centuries, most marriages of young Jewish couples were performed in the home. The venue for the marriage celebration shifted to the synagogue around a millennium ago. In fact the tradition of the groom giving his bride a wedding ring began about the same time; prior to that time, the groom would give the young woman a coin as a symbol of his commitment to her.

It was also about a thousand years ago when the custom prevailed of the newlyweds—right after the ceremony— leaving the wedding party and being alone for a time while the marriage was consummated, gave way to the *chupah*, the wedding canopy, symbol. The so-called bridal chamber rite was not considered seemly by many Jews, for it generally included the groom, or the mothers' of the pair, holding aloft a blood-stained sheet to demonstrate the virginity of the bride. Among some very small groups of Jews, this bloody sheet custom still prevails.

When the ceremony was moved from home to synagogue, it took place in the courtyard. Later, the wedding was held in the synagogue proper, in front of the ark containing the holy Scrolls of the Law, the handwritten parchment versions of the Torah. Some of the more Orthodox Jewish weddings take place on a roof, so as to have God's blessing descend directly on the newlyweds. In the Middle Ages, most brides cut their hair and wore a head covering at all times. This custom, still practiced among very Orthodox Jews, is meant to ensure that the woman will no longer be attractive to any man other than her husband. Such a custom was unknown, however, in biblical times. Ironically, today some of the women who cut their hair and wear a fancy wig instead find that their new head covering makes them more attractive than ever!

CHAPTER TWENTY-ONE

When a New Husband Stayed Home for a Year

In biblical times, a careful reading of the Torah reveals, there was a strong tendency among the Israelites to marry within the clan. Abraham married Sarah, a half-sister; his brother Nahor married a niece; Isaac, Esau, and Jacob all married cousins; Moses' father, Amram, wed his aunt; and Moses himself broke the mold, so to speak, by first marrying a Midianite and then a Cushite. Two of the twelve tribe founders—the sons of Jacob—Judah and Simeon married Canaanite women; and the great Joseph, who rose to become the savior of Egypt in the time of famine and later rescued his own immediate family, married an Egyptian.

By the time we come to Samson, in the biblical narrative, we can almost hear a plea by his parents that has a familiar echo in the closing years of the twentieth century: "Aren't there any suitable Jewish girls around that you have to marry a Gentile?"

The marriage of Abraham to his half-sister Sarah would

not be permitted today under Jewish religious law; the rabbis explain that in those far off days all the laws of marriage had not yet been considered and agreed upon; and besides, inasmuch as Abraham and Sarah had different mothers, it was permissible. Had they had the same father, the rabbis emphasized, it would have been prohibited. Some rabbis explain that in this text, "father" meant grandfather.

The early Hebrews, generally speaking, preferred endogamous marriages, i.e., within the same extended family unit or social grouping. The same preference still seems to exist within the Hasidic movement, where every effort is made to match up the offspring of leaders of the Hasidic followers. From the time that Moses first brought the Torah down from Mount Sinai to the former Hebrew slaves, and began urging that they observe its rules and regulations, he spoke out against intermarriage, i.e., Hebrews with foreign, pagan peoples. Later, after the first Holy Temple was destroyed and the Hebrews were taken captive by the Babylonians, many did wed pagan women; still later, when the Hebrews were allowed to return to the Land of Israel as free men, the prophet Ezra ordered them to shed their foreign wives before returning home, fearing foreign pagan influence. Reluctantly, many did so, but apparently others did not.

The importance of marrying and raising children who would continue the still new beliefs in monotheism remained high on the people's agenda. Priests, who were expected to lead an exemplary pious life and teach the ordinary people how to develop a religious, ethical lifestyle, were not excused from the obligation to marry and raise a family. Some limitations were placed on whom the priests could marry—the wife had to be a virgin, never a divorcee nor a widow. However, if the widow had previously been married to a priest, she was acceptable as a marital partner for the priest.

In an attempt to set up high standards, the rabbis of ancient times ruled that if a wife of an ordinary Hebrew had been captured during a time of war, or by bandits, it had to be assumed that she had had sexual relations with her captors, willingly or otherwise. She could not under the circumstances return to her husband, unless she could prove that she had been raped, or that somehow she had been able to avoid sexual relations while she was a captive. For a priest however the situation was different: even a slight suspicion that his wife had been "defiled" required that she be sent away by her husband.

From biblical times, marriages were arranged by the fathers. However, both the bride and groom had the right to reject the proposed marital partner. The Bible recounts that when Abraham sent Eliezer on his mission to obtain a wife for his son Isaac, he told his servant that "if the woman will not be willing to follow you, then you are absolved from this, my oath."

The custom of the groom's father in those days was to pay a *mohar*, or a bride price, to the bride's father. This generally consisted of fifty shekels of silver. Some grooms, however, were too poor to have a *mohar*; this was the case with Jacob, who proposed instead to work seven years for the right to marry Rachel, a proposal that his father-in-law-to-be, Laban, accepted. Later, as the biblical narrative tells it, Laban tricked Jacob into working for him another seven years and at the same time marrying off his older daughter, Leah, to Jacob.

The dowry—a gift to the bride by her own father on the occasion of her marriage—seemed to have less significance than the *mohar* in those ancient times. The moment that a bride price was paid, the couple was regarded by all as betrothed, a legal first step towards marriage. Usually, the next step in this procedure was for the bride to leave her parents' home and move into the home of the groom. If the prospective husband was the scion of a wealthy family, there generally was a celebration at his parents' home; if he was poor, he would lead her, upon her arrival, to his tent, where the marriage was consummated. Following the consummation, the custom in those days was for the bride's parents to hold aloft the blood-stained bedsheet, to prove that their daughter had been a virgin. This was then followed by the bride's being accepted by the community as a recognized, married woman.

Most men of that era followed the biblical injunction to stay home with their wives for a full year after marriage, and thus smooth out any adjustment problems that might arise for the newlyweds.

* * *

As in many other faiths, Judaism has also experienced major changes in customs, traditions and laws, including all those that relate to the sacred step of marriage. The great Maimonides—rabbi, physician, philosopher—said, a thousand years ago, that a man and woman could live together only with the formal permission of *kiddushin*. This rabbinic term, usually translated as sanctification, is attained by a man "taking" a woman, a step that was achieved in ancient times through one of three ways— only one of which is still observed:

1. *Kessef* (money): The man hands the woman a coin, nowadays a ring, in front of two witnesses and recites the famous phrase uttered under the wedding canopy—"You are hereby betrothed unto me with this ring according to the laws of Moses and Israel." By accepting the ring, the bride accepts and is married to the groom. This is the only widely accepted Jewish marital ceremony today.

2. *Sh'tar* (contract): The man gives the woman, again before two witnesses, a deed, containing the couple's names and the groom's formula for marriage. This deed is designed to lead to a bond of marriage (and should not be confused with the *ketubah*, the marriage contract, which is handed to the bride for her legal protection, after the *kiddushin* rite).

3. *Bi'ah* (intercourse): In this instance, after the husband-to-be has addressed the marriage formula to his wife-to-be, with two witnesses in attendance, the two take off to a private place, and through sexual intercourse seek to effect the betrothal.

This third option was barred by the rabbis in the third century, with one rabbi calling for flogging for any couple who proceeds in this manner. Nonetheless, technically, if such a marriage takes place, it is considered religiously valid.

Thus, nowadays, only the first method of marrying, with the use of the ring as a symbol of commitment, is acceptable and in general use. The other two forms of effecting a marriage are considered as obsolete.

Today's marriage ceremony unites all the elements of the ceremony under the wedding canopy; despite the customs of the past, a couple today may not cohabit until they have been fully married.

Nevertheless, some of the phraseology used in the contemporary Jewish wedding ceremony may be offensive to a modern woman. The Bible, for example, talks of "when a man *acquires* a wife." This word offends some people, harking back to eras of slavery, purchase of people, forcible unions with an innocent young woman. But, as the contemporary rabbis are quick to point out, nothing could be further from the truth than an impression that the man—in a Jewish wedding ceremony—gains a wife in some kind of ancient, totally dated ceremony. One can easily explain the word *acquires* as actually meaning that the husband undertakes an awesome responsibility, namely, providing for a wife, and later for children, and assuming the role of husband and father with all its myriad obligations.

True, on the surface, one might mistakenly assume that the word *acquires* sounds too much like obtaining a piece of property. In a way, there are similarities: When you marry, you tell the world that this woman, whom you love, is consecrated to you and no other; and when you buy real estate and post a sign that the area is off limits, the goal is the same. But Jewish tradition treats women— wives, mothers and sisters, indeed all women—very differently from the way one deals with property. A wife is part of you, spiritually, emotionally; she is your lifelong partner, and even more; from the time of the wedding ceremony, you and she will share everything, the good times and (hopefully not) the bad; if there are children to raise and nurture, it will be the two parents together who will be called upon to do the job.

Indeed, when a couple marries it is imperative that they understand that they are giving up their previous lifestyle, their singleness, their bachelorhood; they embark at that point on a totally new path, in which—in every sense of the term—they become a "we."

Without question, Judaism has always interpreted a marriage as meaning that a husband does not own his wife. She is consecrated unto him just as he is unto her; they are exclusively, mutually reserved for each other. The marriage ceremony, to ensure that there is no misunderstanding, stresses that the woman fully consents, of her own free will, to the marriage.

To ensure that brides were not deceived by unscrupulous grooms, the wedding ceremony which a long time ago could be performed with only the couple and two witnesses present, was gradually expanded to larger numbers, so as to be certain the bride knew exactly what she was agreeing to, when the groom handed her a ring and announced that she was consecrated to him, and that from then on they were husband and wife.

Only a person ignorant of Jewish teaching could even imagine that the word *acquires* has the ring of enslavement, or the purchase of property. After having slaved for the Egyptians under the cruelest of circumstances, the ancient Hebrews programmed into their psyche a distaste for slavery, and the idea of owning another human being became anathema. The annual reading of the Passover Seder service stresses that we who were once slaves must never forget how evil this way of life really is.

In Ethics of the Fathers, that marvelous collection of moral teachings compiled from the Talmud, we are advised to "acquire a friend." It does not mean buy a friend, nor own a friend, but rather work at cultivating friendship; if you are lucky, you will find a good and true friend—and then develop that friendship. The same is true of acquiring a wife: you neither own her, nor buy her. You marry first, and then work at establishing marital relations; just as you must extend yourself to win friends, you must do the same to "win" over your wife.

* * *

There is an erroneous impression in some circles that when a Jewish woman marries a Jewish man, she loses some independence, and that he gains an extra degree of upperhandedness. Not true. A man can divorce his wife in Judaism; and a woman can divorce her husband. For example, to demonstrate the individuality of both marriage partners: although it is certainly true that when husband and wife marry, they are bound to each other, in total, mutual commitment. But, if the woman sins or does something criminal, she is responsible, not he. They remain separate, individual people. And the same of course is true if he sins or does something criminal; then he is responsible.

If, however, the wife acts irrational or carries on immorally in public then the husband has the right and the duty to intervene, and try to help her. The Jewish view about adultery is not that a man's "property" has been violated, but that the wife, by her actions, has transgressed not against her husband but against God.

Even a thousand years ago, Judaism's insights into women's problems were crystal clear. If a woman complained to the rabbi or rabbinical court that her husband was "objectionable" and that she could not tolerate living with him and could not "willingly agree to be intimate with him," she had every expectation that the husband would be compelled to grant her a divorce. Maimonides explained, "she is not a captive to be compelled to intimacy with someone she hates."

Two of the outstanding authorities of recent centuries ruled: "The woman's person is not acquired by the husband and the marriage ceremony is not a property transaction." (Rashba, in 13th century Spain). The Ramban, also known as Nachmanides, who lived in Spain in the same period, taught that a married woman "has never been the property of her husband and is in her own possession."

Wife-battering, a common and of course reprehensible phenomenon in both the western and eastern worlds, was practically unknown in Jewish families. The marriage contract stipulates that the husband was to honor and love his wife, "as Jewish men are accustomed to do." In the rare instance of a husband beating his wife, she could immediately sue for divorce and maintenance.

The Bible early on stipulated that a husband had no legal claim on his wife's personal finances. What's more the wife, throughout Jewish history, had the right to own property in her own name, and the equally important right to go to work. Indeed, during the Middle Ages especially, the wife was often the major breadwinner. Partly this was because the restrictions that local communities issued against Jews entering various occupations often did not apply to women. The field of money lending, which was often the only occupation open to Jews, had many women involved in it; in some cases, women proved to be so skillful in handling funds that local Jewish charities appointed them to supervise communal funds for the needy.

In later years, however, although the rabbis guaranteed the married woman the right to work, they ruled that her earnings must go to the family's joint fund, in order to assure smooth relations between husband and wife. If, however, she decided to give up her husband's income, she could then keep her own earnings. The primary goal in this ruling was to bolster the concept of *shalom bayit*—a peaceful household.

*   *   *

The *kiddushin* part of the wedding ceremony does not complete the service. The second part is known as *nisu'in*, usually translated as nuptials. Standing under the *chupah*, the wedding canopy representing their future home together, the groom hands the bride the ring, and with the help of the rabbi (although the official can also be a cantor; he must also be recognized by the state in which the service is being held) the groom recites those few magical words that will bind the two people together in marriage. The ceremony under the *chupah* ends with the groom's smashing of a glass underfoot, a reminder of the destruction of the Holy Temple, never to be forgotten even on this day, the couple's happiest. Then, amid shouts of *mazel tov* and applause from the guests, the newlyweds proceed to a private room for a brief period of *yichud*—private togetherness (with two attendants standing by to make sure they are not disturbed). And then, when they emerge from their private room, to join the guests and proceed with the handshakes and kisses and good wishes, they are husband and wife—a wholly new designation that will take time for them to get used to.

Generally, the rabbis explain, the two parts of the wedding service are first, *kiddushin*, referring to the legal bond that now links the couple. The woman must now see herself as a married woman; the second part of the ceremony, *nisu'in*, is more of a religious service on top of the legal tie between the couple. The newlyweds are now expected to consummate their marriage, and bear in mind as they do the Bible's first command: "Be fruitful and multiply." The first term is derived from the Hebrew word for holy, signifying that the marriage of these two people has been hallowed. The second term, *nisu'in*, stems from the Hebrew term meaning elevation, indicating that now the husband and wife have been elevated to a new plane, in a permanent commitment with God.

Judaism sees marriage as a holy relationship, linked to religion and the community. Thus, just as the Jewish people regards its link to God as a covenant, so the Jewish marriage is also seen as a covenant. In other words, anyone can draw up a contract—when you buy a car, for example. But a lifetime marriage, in Jewish tradition, is blessed in the same spirit as is God's covenant with the Jewish people.

As Rabbi Lamm writes: "By contract, we share duties; by covenant we share destinies."

One overriding characteristic that many people overlook at a Jewish wedding is the absolutely firm need to obtain the bride's agreement to the marriage. The rabbis argued that it is the groom who generally proposes marriage but it must be the bride who willingly and without pressure of any kind agrees to get married. Otherwise, the rabbis ruled, if she subsequently complained that she has been coerced, and did not of her own free will enter the marriage on a positive note, then the marriage could be declared null and void, without waiting for a formal divorce. A woman who becomes a bride must without any doubt whatsoever consent to the wedding. This is a hard and fast rule.

The relatively short but deeply meaningful ceremony held under the *chupah* must be attended by two witnesses. They cannot, by Jewish law, be relatives, close or distant. Preferably they should be observant Jews who are individuals of integrity and learning. Their chief function under the wedding canopy is to see clearly the groom put the ring on the bride's finger, and to hear him recite the words of commitment to her. They must also see the bride accept the ring willingly, and by her smile and body language they should be able to tell that she is getting married willingly and happily.

* * *

The Torah, in matters of marriage, has acted to protect certain categories of men and women who might otherwise be taken advantage of. Certain laws about marriage have evolved over the years to protect the interests of the deaf-mute, the retarded person, the deranged and the minor. This is a whole, special and quite complex body of Jewish law that requires careful discussion with a rabbi competent in this area. In recent years, as enormous medical advances have been made, some of the rulings have been altered. It is best, when confronted with this very special situation, to make a thorough investigation of the latest responsa, that is, replies to religious questions that cover this particular problem.

In the same vein, one other special area of concern that should be checked out when a couple wishes to marry is the unique problem of what are known as "Jewish genetic diseases." Here too one must find competent physicians familiar with this phenomenon, which thankfully is not widespread but which can be devastating if not dealt with.

CHAPTER TWENTY-TWO

Enjoying Life Is a Religious Commandment

To a cynic, the word *love* is an oxymoron; it is meaningless. He sees the world through black lenses—everything is negative, people are basically bad, there is nothing and no one in whom to believe. Life, in other words, says the cynic, is a ridiculous charade; only money and the satisfaction of one's baser lusts are worthwhile. Such a person is to be pitied; he is alive, but inside his soul—assuming he possesses one—is dead.

A believing Jew, no matter how lax he may be in his observance of Jewish religious law, knows deep in his heart that life is good, it is meant to be lived fully and enjoyably, and all good things are meant to be shared with our fellow human beings. Can anyone fail to react to the words that Anne Frank wrote, when she and her family were locked up in a secret room, in the midst of the Nazi madness: "Despite everything, I believe in the basic decency of people."

When two people set out to get married, to link their

lives together and fashion a new family, to have and raise children, to confront the world from that point on as a married couple, it is because they love each other, and because they believe that love is a beautiful, eternal concept that will enhance their lives, and give it a whole new and happy dimension. As Rabbi Aryeh Kaplan wrote: "Love and lust should not be confused. Love wants to give, lust only wants to take. Love is reciprocal... one identifies with the wants and needs of the beloved."

In Hebrew numerology, known as *gematriah*, the Hebrew word for love (*ahavah*) adds up numerically to thirteen. The same number comes up for the Hebrew word for one (*echad*). Thus, say the mystics of old, what love does is take two people and forge them into one.

Love between a man and a woman is a term that is very difficult to define. Parental love, love of God, love of country—those are relatively easy to explain. But a man's love for a woman, or her love for him—we know what it is when we see it, but somehow it defies rational definition. To really know what love is, a person must be in love; there is no other way to know.

The *Song of Songs* in the Bible has been treasured for centuries as a stirring, beautiful volume of poetry describing passionate love between a man and a woman. There are commentators who insist that it is really an allegory of the love that exists between God and humanity, or between God and the Jewish people. But what many fail to see in the ancient words is that it is also a remarkable tribute to love itself. The words spell out movingly the pain of separation between two people in love, as well as the joys of closeness between them when they are together.

When a young man and a young woman are planning to marry, perhaps it would be a good idea for them to read (or reread) the *Song of Songs*, and in doing so determine if they discover, during the course of reading the ancient text, if they find themselves thinking of their respective mates-to-be. That would be a good sign, in all likelihood, that the match is a good one. And perhaps as they study the millennia-old words they will come to the realization that the idea of love is a divine gift, meant to be enjoyed and shared. But of course this heaven-sent gift of love must be pure, selfless, and appreciated as a rare and unique phenomenon.

*   *   *

The Talmudic sages, a long time ago, understood the love of a man and a woman. "One's wife is like one's own body," one tractate asserts. When there is perfect love between a man and a woman, they become like a single, unified person, says another Talmudic commentator. Another rabbi noted the biblical phrase stating that "God created the human in His image, in the image of God He created them, male and female He created them"—the rabbi pointed out that neither the man nor the woman is in the image of God, until the Bible speaks of them as male and female; in other words, it is only when the man and woman are harmoniously together, i.e., married, that they form "the image of God."

Judaism describes God in many different ways; one of them is as the Creator. Instinctively a person knows that he or she too becomes like the Creator when they marry and have a child; after all, is there any act that a man and a woman can do together that is more noble, more majestic, more God-like than creating another human being? Which is why some Talmudic sages explain when a child is born, the new parents may feel themselves to be partners with the Creator Himself.

In another of the Bible's volumes, the book of Proverbs,

attributed to the wise King Solomon, he is quoted as having taught that a man who "finds a wife, finds good." Later in life, when he was considerably older, Solomon—purportedly the author also of Ecclesiastes—took a more severe attitude towards life, and taught there that one should "enjoy life with the woman you love."

The gift of love, in Jewish tradition, is one of God's greatest boons to humanity. It enables a man and a woman to join together to form a family, and the family in turn will be—like families through the millennia—a foundation stone for humanity's future.

*   *   *

In the closing years of the violence-prone twentieth century, during which tens of millions of people were slaughtered in the course of two catastrophic world wars, and in almost countless smaller wars, and of course during the Holocaust—against the backdrop of so much senseless and evil bloodletting, young couples come along and say, in effect: "Everything is nil. Nothing has any moral value. If I want to live with someone, that's my business. Why does religion have to get involved? And if the law of the land says I have to get married, in order to enjoy the benefits of health insurance and similar benefits, why can't we just get married with a judge or a justice of the peace? Who needs all this wedding hoopla?"

When young people are willful, and deliberately set out to reject a Jewish religious ceremony, there usually is not much that can be said to influence them otherwise. Of course, if one partner is not Jewish then the Jewish wedding ceremony will only be presided over by a small number of Reform rabbis; most Orthodox and Conservative rabbis will not even recognize it as a lawful marriage. And should the couple ever wish to come to Israel as

Jewish immigrants, such a marriage would be rejected and they would not be considered bona fide Jews.

On the other hand, if both the young man and the young woman are Jews and they insist on living together without benefit of a religious wedding ceremony, or they wish a civil marriage to suffice for them, then the situation is somewhat different: Under these circumstances, Judaism teaches, the original civil marriage or the history of the couple living together as though they were married (in other words it was a common law arrangement) are disregarded; it is as though they never took place. In fact, if such a couple wishes to separate and obtain a divorce, they do not require a religious *get* inasmuch as they were never legally wed in a Jewish ceremony. There are decisors (learned specialists in the fine nuances of Jewish law) who believed that a common law arrangement really means that the woman is a concubine, and therefore has no legal rights to the man's estate, in the event of his death. There are some legal authorities who say that in such a common law arrangement, should the couple decide to separate, she could, legally, turn around and marry one of his best friends or relatives, and it would all be regarded as perfectly kosher. In other words, a cohabiting Jewish couple that rejects Jewish religious law, i.e., the "law of Moses and Israel," cannot benefit from those same legal provisions which are meant to protect the couple throughout their lifetime.

There are Jewish couples who live together for a number of years without benefit of marriage. Like other couples, sometimes they are happy, sometimes not. Chances are overwhelming that the parents of the couple would be infinitely happier if they were wed in a traditional Jewish religious ceremony; however, since in most cases the young people involved are in their adult years, they cannot be coerced nor persuaded to take the marital step.

What does happen, however, is that the young woman gets pregnant; then a new factor enters the situation, and the couple—in the vast majority of cases—wants the child-to-come to have the same benefits of married parents as the other kids enjoy; that is when in many cases the couple marries. Generally, it is a quiet ceremony held in the rabbi's study with only the immediate family in attendance; quite often the bride is visibly pregnant. Everyone, almost always, acts very grownup and sophisticated, and the couple—after five or ten or more years of cohabitation—stands under the wedding canopy, and emerges as man and wife.

In biblical Jewish law, having sexual relations with the intent of getting married is an acceptable way of establishing a Jewish family. The emphasis is on the intent. Thus, when we look upon the relatively large number of young Jewish couples who live together without benefit of a religious wedding ceremony, the question arises as to the couple's intentions: Do they look forward to getting married in the future? Are they just trying out living together before they decide to take that step? Are they perhaps a bit immature in the sense that they believe not being married means they are still young? Are they still battling their parents with some of the same hostility they mustered during their growing-up teens?

These are of course difficult questions to answer. Most rabbis when consulted by the parents of these unmarried, living-together Jewish couples advise patience; in the course of time, the parents are told, a marriage will take place.

Various states in the United States have different laws with respect to these common-law marriages. If a couple lives together for X-number of years, the state's law declares, they are considered married. However, there is no uniform federal law on the subject.

* * *

Another characteristic of the closing years of the twentieth century is the growing number of Jewish couples looking to adoption for the simple reason that either she or he is having trouble producing a child. Why? There are many possible explanations, but one of them is that more and more couples are getting married at later ages. And although it is true that modern science and advanced medicine have enabled mothers even in their early forties to give birth to healthy children, it is still true that a younger couple has a far better chance to have healthy children. Another reason for the surge in adoptions is the growing awareness among more knowledgeable Jewish couples of the existence of Jewish genetic diseases—conditions that may turn out to produce a child with serious physical or emotional defects. (If one marital partner carries the gene, it is not as risky, of course; but if both do, the risk is quite high.)

Judaism looks upon adoption as an opportunity to give a deprived child a happy home and a good future, as well as to fill a childless Jewish home with the energy, joy and sparkle of a child. It has become more and more usual to see young American Jewish couples introducing their children at the Passover seder, at synagogue services, at Chanukah parties and the like, and to notice immediately that the children in question often are Asian or Latin-American, for these are children most easily available for adoption.

Jewish law requires that a non-Jewish infant must be converted to Judaism at the time of adoption. This means that a small male child has to undergo circumcision and a small female child has a brief ceremony of conversion that takes place in a *mikvah*, a ritual bath. Of course Jewish law explicitly states that an adopted child, once converted to Judaism, is regarded as fully Jewish.

A unique development in recent years among Hasidic and Orthodox Jews has affected adoption policies. Because Orthodox Jews are fearful of adopting a Jewish child, or someone who might stem from a Jewish biological parent, lest somewhere down the line there might be a situation where such a child would inadvertently marry a close blood relative—which is forbidden, of course—they prefer to seek out Asian or other children, where there is no such possibility.

Many great figures in Jewish history were adopted children. One of these was the noted Talmudic scholar Abbaye. There have been many others. One case that comes to mind is of a relative who had trouble conceiving and decided to adopt a motherless little girl; later, she did give birth and was heard to complain, "I wish my own daughter would be half as nice as the one I adopted!"

One stumbling block that frequently arises when a Jewish couple seeks to adopt a non-Jewish child through an American social agency is a request by the birth mother to have the adoptive parents raise the child in a Christian home. Social agencies handling such cases of course are required by law to abide by the biological mother's wishes. There are not that many Jewish biological mothers ready to give up their children for adoption to Jewish families, which is one reason why so many Jewish couples go abroad to find a suitable young child for adoption.

Sometimes the adoptions are very poignant. A young relative and her husband decided to adopt after they realized that the wife could not have a child; she had tried unsuccessfully but her age was against her. They traveled to China, made all the arrangements and returned with a beautiful, bright little girl. The first thing they did was arrange for a religious conversion ceremony. Then she was named in the synagogue—this lovely little Asian child, now a Jewish little girl, has a first and a middle name; they are Sarah and Hannah, and are in memory of the adoptive grandfather's sisters, who were murdered in the Holocaust.

CHAPTER TWENTY-THREE

Making a Marriage Happy And Fulfilling

With divorce rates at an all-time high, with millions of people in the western world seemingly constantly on the lookout for easy panaceas for every conceivable problem in life, is it any wonder that young men and women about to get married seek out anyone who will advise them on how to have a happy marriage? We live in an age of instant gratification—from instant cereals to instant computer-provided retrieval systems. So, these young people about to plunge into marriage ask—how can we be sure it will be a happy relationship? Are there any courses to take, books to read, tapes to listen to? Come on, they seem to be saying, Judaism has been around for a very long time; it is without doubt a very wise religion, it must have the answers—how do we have a great marriage?

Pragmatically and realistically, Jewish teaching says that love between husband and wife is not something to be considered, it is something to be done. If there is scant love between the mates, the ethical teacher of the eighteenth century, Rabbi Eliezer Papo, taught, it becomes "obligatory for husband and wife to love each other." Another ethical teacher, Rabbi Eliyahu Dessler, said: "In every act and in every thought, one is either taking or giving. This corrupted world is filled with takers despoiling and exploiting each other... but the perfect world is one where every person gives to others—a happy society overflowing with peace and love."

In a successful marriage, Judaism teaches, the marital partners must give freely, selflessly to one another. This marital style of giving is nothing more than a continuation of a parent's giving to a child, or of God's giving to His creations. Once a couple marries, they recognize a new status—they are no longer independent but rather mutually dependent. When a husband and a wife come to realize that their new status means each is now required to consider the other at all times, this new realization will bring in its wake a sense of selfless giving that will lead to pure love, which in turn is the surest basis for a happy marriage.

Rabbi Samson Raphael Hirsch, commenting on Isaac and Rebecca's nuptials in the Bible, noted that "the more she became his wife, the more he loved her.... Successful Jewish marriages are contracted not by passion but by reason and judgment. Such marriages keep growing, the more they get to know each other."

Besides, one may ask, what really is meant by a "happy marriage"? We know what marriage is—but what's happy? Many years ago, the mother of one of the authors of this volume was hospitalized. She had lost her coordination; for a time she could not do a simple thing like return a coffee cup to a saucer. The neurologist who was observing her came up to her one day, and while taking her pulse, asked, "Are you happy?" She shot right back,

"Are you happy, doctor?" To which he responded: "I have six children—I have to be happy!"

Isn't happiness a relative term? If we are happy, are we really happy always, or just sometimes? Does happiness develop slowly as we get older, and presumably wiser? There is a Hasidic comment about happiness "While we pursue happiness, we flee from contentment." And then the book of Proverbs observes: "The miserable man is unhappy every day but the cheerful man constantly enjoys a feast." Ecclesiasticus wrote that "one day's happiness makes a man forget his misfortune, and one day's misfortune makes him forget his happiness." So, is happiness in marriage a will-of-the-wisp, an excuse for not buckling down to making marriage work—by actively, consciously providing one another with love, confidence, strength, and in so doing receiving the benefit of such action?

To encourage men to marry, the Talmudic sages taught that a "beautiful wife makes for happiness and her husband's days are doubled." But men are also cautioned in Jewish tradition "not to make women weep, for God counts their tears."

*   *   *

We return to the original question: How to make a marriage successful? Is there a ready formula?

To try to come up with a meaningful answer, we must backtrack to the original reasons for getting married. These, in Jewish tradition, can be summarized as follows: A person is not regarded as whole unless he is married. Marriage adds a whole new dimension to life—it gives the marital partner a physical outlet and a wholesome link to a member of the opposite sex; emotionally, marriage enables the newlyweds to calm down, for now they are not alone in the world, they are a couple, like all mature couples, a "we" that is acceptable and respected; and there is another aspect to marriage that cannot be dismissed—in the course of time, the newlyweds come to recognize that there is growing up between them a spiritual life that they did not know before, that is making them aware they had been missing out on this spiritual addition to their lives, which is according them a deeper understanding of themselves and of life itself.

When a man and a woman marry, they find release for the sex drive that is universally recognized as very powerful. When they marry, they find companionship; most people are not loners, they enjoy socializing with other people, and being together with one's spouse—assuming of course that they enjoy each other's company—is the highest form of socializing. The emotional problems of loneliness—in a good marriage—evaporate; in addition to which, as time goes on, the spousal relationship grows ever stronger and fills the marital partners' emotional needs.

When a Jewish couple marries, and by tradition or conviction, is determined to conduct their new status in the age-old Jewish mold, they soon come to realize that they are not only enjoying a Jewish way of life but they are also actively helping to carry on the continuity of the Jewish people into the next generation and the generations that follow. Somehow, this young family's way of life takes hold, and the newlyweds swiftly come to sense that they are part of a vast, divine plan for the Jewish people and for mankind as a whole—and, most importantly, they are very much a part of it. This realization brings on that spirituality that so many people seem to be reaching out for, in the final years of the twentieth century.

Aharon Feldman, in his charming book on successful marriage, *The River, the Kettle, and The Bird*, writes that "marriage is not an immediate ticket to spiritual perfection...most of mankind is afflicted by selfish obsessions despite being married. If one chooses to use marriage properly, marriage can make a reorientation of man's aims possible...without a wife and family, man would have little hope of redeeming himself from his spiritual wasteland...true Jewish life is suffused with spiritual values which cannot flourish without marriage."

* * *

"Life, liberty and the pursuit of happiness"... these three are inalienable rights, the founding fathers of the United States proclaimed. And for more than two hundred years, America has stood fast by its belief in these basic principles.

Judaism and its teachings are not known as a religion of joy, but they should be so described. Permeating every aspect of Jewish life—religious, cultural, everyday—is a sense that life is meant to be lived fully in order to achieve happiness. And marriage, Judaism says, is a vital key towards happiness.

Perhaps Judaism never achieved a reputation as a joyous celebration of life because the ancient Hebrews and later the Jews were so often subjected to brutal massacres and assaults. Whatever the reason, we need only open the nearest copy of the Hebrew Bible, and we find the immortal philosopher Ecclesiastes, known in Hebrew as Kohelet, who is purportedly King Solomon, in the final years of his life.

The strongest drive in mankind's nature, he said, was the pursuit of happiness; and since God created man, then it must be He who rooted this goal in our hearts. He takes this a step further and says that ergo, if we are to fulfill God's plan for mankind, we must take it upon ourselves to satisfy this most fundamental of mankind's wishes. The enjoyment of life, therefore, in his teaching is a Divine imperative; and one can easily add, getting married, raising a family, thus become part and parcel of fulfilling God's wishes.

Kohelet wrote:

> There is no greater good for man than eating and drinking, and giving himself joy in his labor. Here is what I have discovered...it is proper for a man to enjoy himself in return for the toil he undergoes under the sun in the scant years God has given him, for that is man's portion and not long will he remember the days of his life. Indeed, every man to whom God has given wealth and possessions and granted the power to enjoy them, that is the gift of God, for it is God who provides him with the joy in his heart.
>
> Therefore, I praise joy, for there is no other good for man under the sun but to eat, drink and be joyful and have this accompany him in his toil, during the days of his life, which God has given beneath the sun.
>
> Enjoy life with the woman whom you love, through all the vain days of your life, which God has given you... throughout your brief days, for that is your reward in life, for your toil under the sun.*

The strong emphasis in Ecclesiastes on everyone's need to enjoy life to the fullest is echoed in other basic Jewish texts. A careful reading of the Hebrew Bible shows that in Psalms, for example, there is frequent reference to the need of people to be *ashrai*, or happy. True, the "happy" references talk of people who fear God, or whose lives are without sinfulness, but this can also easily be interpreted as a round-about way of encouraging people to lead their

Translated by Robert Gordis in "The Wisdom of Ecclesiastes."

lives in accordance with the ancient rules and traditions of Judaism—and that of course includes being married, and making the marriage one that is cast in a Jewish mold.

Ben Sira, in the Apocrypha, millennia ago, taught that "if you have the means, treat yourself well, for there is no pleasure in the grave, and there is no postponement of death." It is inconceivable, in the Jewish heritage, for a man or a woman to go through life and not marry; and those who do marry and are not blessed with children are to be pitied. Life, in short, is meant to be lived to the fullest, and enjoyed—but always in the path laid down so many centuries ago by the sages of the Jewish people.

Rabbis are fond of telling a story of an elderly Jew who died and went to "the other world." The descendant was certain he would be welcomed warmly and given comfortable facilities, so that when he was escorted to a modest shack by the angels, he was taken aback.

Obviously upset, he protested: "Don't I deserve better than this? All my life wasn't I kind, compassionate and charitable?"

One of the angels replied immediately, "Yes, you were all those things but we were ordered to assign you this place because"—the angel paused—"we were told when you lived on earth, you did not take advantage of all the beautiful things that are there, you didn't enjoy yourself as you should have. And that is a sin, so this is where you go."

Two Talmudic sages made the same point. Samuel taught that we should "seize hold and eat, seize hold and drink, for this world whence we depart is like a wedding feast." Rab declared that "every man must render an account before God of all the good things he beheld in life and did not enjoy."

In sharp contradiction to other religious faiths, the majority view in Judaism through the ages has been to take hold of life with two hands—with all its difficulties, frustrations and challenges—and transform the experience into a life of happiness. And without a wife or a husband, to share both life's troubles and life's joys, the struggle is an empty one. The English essayist Francis Bacon wrote what he thought was a criticism of Judaism: "Prosperity is the blessing of the Old Testament; adversity of the New." But Jews accepted his judgment, for they believe that prosperity is a gift of God, to be enjoyed by all.

And yet, no sensible or sensitive reader can avoid the feeling that dominates society in this age: Something is very wrong. Divorce, regarded by most people as a great tragedy, is on the rise. Extramarital affairs are on the rise. Sexually transmitted diseases, which were thought to have been vanquished, are back and increasing. Many people, and probably most people, do not seem to be happy, content, satisfied. There is a restlessness and threat of violence that hovers over almost every segment of society. A great many people marry, and half of them get divorced in relatively short order. And a great many people move in together, and live together without the traditional marriage ceremony—and they too, after a while, separate and split up.

So, what's wrong? For Jewish young people, does Judaism have some guidelines that will make marriage attractive, and when they marry lead to a life of permanence and genuine happiness? Can such nuggets of wisdom also be adopted by non-Jewish couples?

CHAPTER TWENTY-FOUR

The New Problems Facing Jewish Families

Commentators nowadays talk a good deal about the new morality. The term is all-inclusive and certainly indicates that women, having received a vast array of new rights in politics, employment, and other areas, now also wish to be accorded equal rights in matters marital and sexual. Fine—but just a moment: has the new morality and the granting of new rights to women led to a stabler society, or to a more anxious and more troubled community?

There is another point to consider: In traditional Judaism, there is no such thing as a difference between sex and love. They are one and the same, and are meant to be enjoyed in a stable, loving, marital relationship. In western society, which of course is a Christian society, in the late 1990s, love and sex have been separated. The husband-wife relationship is for love, and the other relationships are often, although not always, for sexual pleasure.

Not that such things did not go on in previous centuries. They certainly did. But in our era, with the development of new social and economic realities for women, and with the evolvement of easily available birth control methods, the new morality has come into its own. Many people do not even blush when they talk of their adult children living together with members of the opposite sex without benefit of marriage. It has become de rigueur, chic, stylish.

Has this new wrinkle in society produced a happier generation? Or, quite the contrary, are more people seemingly less happy than they were a generation ago? Tough questions.

While we contemplate the new state of affairs, we must not err about the past. Nostalgia has a way of skipping all the bad chapters in human history and just focusing on the good. But the truth is that in past centuries, both among Jews and non-Jews, there were unhappy marriages, sick wives, overworked mothers, frustrated husbands, tyrannized spouses, and whole generations of youngsters who grew up in abject poverty and misery. Generations ago, when women in many cases did not even have an opportunity to learn to read and write, what kind of life did they have? How many of those illiterate women lived and died before they could determine if they had talent and skills that might benefit or entertain society?

Generations ago, before the advent of electricity and all those marvelous labor-saving devices that modern families accept today as their due, how many women, and men, too, died prematurely of fatigue, disease, and sheer boredom? Thus, all those macho men who like to talk of the "good old days" are not rushing back to those days, when men worked long and hard hours, and their span of life hovered around forty or maybe fifty. And in the Jewish community, too, those nostalgia-breathing Jews refrain from returning to the "good old *shtetl* days" because deep in their hearts they know they weren't so good.

Nevertheless, the new age in which we live has produced a so-called new morality, and it must be seen and confronted. Is it not really our young people's reaction to a nuclear-threatened world? Do they not reach out for "fun" because of the constant threat of global war and destruction? and in reaching out, do they not reach out to each other, i.e., a young man to a young woman, and vice-versa, looking for love, comfort, companionship? And do they not shy away from marriage in so many cases because they are fearful of the future?

This then is a time when we must be particularly compassionate and understanding of our children. If it is not an easy time for parents who would like to see their sons and daughters marry in a traditional manner, neither is it an easy time for the young people themselves. If ever there was a need for understanding between the generations, it certainly is now.

* * *

In attempting to cope with the new problems confronting young Jewish couples nowadays vis-a-vis ancient Jewish marriage laws and customs which may seem archaic to some, Judaism says in effect: Look, we are a religion and a culture and a way of life that dates back close to four thousand years. During our long history, we have learned a thing or two. One must remember that we started out as a nomadic, desert people ruled by a patriarchal system, and then we went on to a more urban civilization and also with established agricultural villages. Side by side with the once-great empires of the Orient, Egypt, Assyria, and Babylonia, and later the Greek and Roman worlds, Jewish civilization evolved. It adapted, it grew, it learned from its surroundings and its neighbors, and continued on through the Middle Ages and the modern era. Judaism has witnessed slave economies in the ancient world, feudalism and repression in the medieval era, and modern capitalism as well as modern communism. Its basic teachings and tenets have not been altered; they have been expanded to coincide with changing times, and in some instances certain practices have been allowed to drop away and become obsolete.

To understand Jewish marriage, one must first understand Judaism. Although some theologians, as well as some politicians, especially during election periods, like to talk of the Judeo-Christian tradition as though it is essentially identical, and certainly there are many areas of similarity, the fact is there are fundamental, vital differences between the two faiths. Judaism regards marriage, and includes the sexual aspect of marriage, as a gift from God, and as a positive factor in life. Jews see celibacy as an unnatural way of life, and as a direct refutation of God's command in the early pages of the Bible that we should "be fruitful and multiply and fill the earth."

Further, Judaism has a very distinctive approach to sexual morality, and holds strongly that sex and love are to be united in marriage, and that they are divine gifts meant to bring joy to mankind, as well as to raise a new generation. What's more, Judaism holds, sex and love cannot be divided; they are, or should be, one.

The Jewish world view, as it were, sees all contemporary problems and challenges from a historical vantage point. Throughout our long history many other challenges and tough issues have arisen, and we have survived because we looked at them through a Jewish-historical prism. And as the Bible teaches, there is nothing really new under the sun; some of these difficult challenges—perhaps in another form—have been around before. As the philosopher-rabbi Robert Gordis wrote, "Jewish tradition (may be described as) growth is the law of life, and law is the life of Judaism."

In other words, during this long, long historical period, Judaism has continued to grow, to adjust, to adapt, all the time remaining true to its original laws and teachings. That, essentially, is the secret of Jewish survival. Historians will point to the fact that when the Jewish people resided in their own country, they demonstrated a creative talent in producing great works of learning; later, after they were exiled and scattered and lived in medieval Europe, their positive attitude towards marital sex came into conflict to some extent with ascetic Christian neighbors, and this influenced the Jews somewhat.

By the time we arrived in our own era, Jewish teaching about marriage could be described as basically traditional, encapsulating ancient biblical mores but influenced to some extent by the world through which the Jews had passed, especially in the two millennia of exile that began in the year 70. Thus, although the Bible mentioned en passant a wedding ceremony that was followed by a celebration, the modern Jewish wedding incorporated the ceremony and the celebration that followed, as well as the fancy dress-up clothes that the Jews saw their neighbors wear during their wedding parties.

There is also for example, a brief reference in the Bible to a procession during a wedding ceremony, which has become part and parcel of most modern Jewish wedding ceremonies. However, at Christian weddings there are also bridesmaids and ushers; so, modern Jewish wedding ceremonies have made them a part of the Jewish wedding, too.

This long chain of history includes one aspect that is little known to modern Jewish women. Although it is true that from earliest times men in Judaism seemed to be the dominant sex in matters of inheritance, divorce and other legislation, the fact is that slowly but steadily the rights of women have been brought up to virtually an equal status. This is important to remember when one hears young Jewish women claim that they are resisting having a Jewish wedding because they do not wish to be made to feel inferior. They could not be more wrong.

*   *   *

One of the most heart-wrenching problems confronting Jewish families is a planned intermarriage, i.e., a marriage between their Jewish child and a non-Jewish person who has no intention of converting to Judaism. Many Christians find the Jewish attitude, in most cases, hard to fathom. After all, a Catholic marrying a Protestant hardly causes a ripple. But a Jew marrying out of the faith seems to be a cataclysmic event.

The explanation for this is not difficult to grasp. Fifty years ago, one out of every three Jewish men, women and children in the world was deliberately massacred by the Nazis and their cohorts, while the world at large did not lift a hand to prevent this Holocaust. Jews see in a Jew marrying out a posthumous victory for Hitler. They have the same reaction when their child, or grandchild, announces that he is leaving the Jewish community and converting to the Christian faith in order to marry a Christian partner. The same reaction follows if a Jewish young person joins a group like Jews for Jesus, or winds up in some kind of cultic group. It's really quite simple— we simply don't want to lose any more members of the Jewish community.

It should also be emphasized that Judaism never was and still is not a proselytizing faith. We do not seek to influence non-Jews to leave their own faith and become Jewish, but if they choose to do so, of their own volition, they are welcomed and accepted wholeheartedly.

There is something of a misconception among non-Jews

that converting to Judaism is a very difficult and daunting task. It really is not; basically, conversion (for a female) requires a certain period of study of Jewish religious beliefs, and a fundamental knowledge of Jewish history, and the study period (usually a year) is followed by a brief ceremony in the *mikvah*. For a man the same study requirement applies and this is then followed by a circumcision or, in many cases, a kind of make-believe symbolic circumcision ceremony. It is certainly best for a would-be convert to consult a rabbi for the precise rulings, which do vary from rabbi to rabbi.

Converting to Judaism should not of course be undertaken lightly. In the first place, the law states quite clearly that if someone wishes to convert to Judaism in order to marry a Jewish person, such a conversion is not acceptable. The truth is however that a great many converts do become Jewish for just that reason, but keep their intention hidden from the rabbi conducting conversion classes. Most rabbis, nonetheless, can easily determine the reason behind a conversion; they seldom make a fuss. From experience the rabbis have learned that a very large proportion of the converts turn out to be exemplary Jews, often putting born Jews to shame by their more active participation in synagogue services and programs

One of the real problems with conversion that is painful to observe is the reaction of the convert's family, before he takes that step and after. Many Christian families still bear ancient prejudices against Jews which may have been handed down to them from older generations—despite the fact that they themselves had never known a Jew, and usually know nothing about Judaism.

A family in the synagogue of which we are members had a son-in-law who had converted to Judaism and became a much-loved member of the extended family. Unexpectedly things happened. After a dozen years, the young man and his wife decided to separate and divorce; everyone who knew them was shocked and deeply saddened. The young man, the convert to Judaism, had a particularly warm relationship with his father-in-law. After the divorce, no one in the congregation had the heart to ask Mr. "M" about his ex-son-in-law: How were the relations between them now? Was the son-in-law still Jewish?

One rabbi told a story of a young man in his synagogue who had met a young Gentile girl; they were in love and planned to marry, and the young woman planned to convert to Judaism. She came to see the rabbi to make arrangements, and he began to ask some questions. It turned out that the young woman's mother had been Jewish because her mother—the grandmother—had been Jewish. Both the grandmother and the mother had married non-Jews, and the young woman assumed she needed to convert. When the rabbi told her that according to Jewish religious law she was Jewish and there was no need to convert, she almost fainted. Although she had never before set foot in a synagogue, and although she had never celebrated a Jewish holiday or observed any Jewish law or custom, she was Jewish by virtue of the fact that her mother was Jewish.

The moral is very simple: A person who opts to convert to Judaism is taking a huge step. He or she must be sure that this major change in identity is what is really wanted, and must be ready to accept the negative reactions that are sure to come from some friends and relatives.

It works the other way too. A Jewish young man or woman who wishes to surrender their faith and formally become a practicing Christian must be sure; they too must study the tenets of the new religion and feel certain they agree with its teachings. And they must be ready to accept negative reactions from friends and family.

Most important, in either case, a would-be convert must understand that by marrying into another faith and converting into that faith, they are not merely marrying one person, but they are becoming part of a whole community, a whole different civilization, essentially a whole different way of life.

* * *

What then does Judaism have to say about marriage?

First, Judaism stresses that the search for personal happiness is a perfectly honorable and legitimate lifetime ambition. In addition to its role in procreation, Judaism teaches, sexual pleasure within marriage is a positive, acceptable pursuit both for the husband and wife. Second, the goal of marriage is to produce a new generation, and another goal is to provide the couple with lifetime love and companionship. Third, the need for equality between men and women in the Jewish community is an ongoing challenge, although it should be recognized that great strides have been made in this area. Fourth, marital partners must observe mutual respect and must also allow each partner's individual personality to grow and flourish. Fifth, the married couple should approach their married life believing that sex in marriage is not sinful, and that marriage itself is not a jailhouse, and divorce—if it ever became an option—is not a crime.

And since marriage is so fundamental to a person's well-being—physically, emotionally, spiritually—every effort should be made to make every marriage happy and successful.

Epilogue

Some 2,600 years ago, following the destruction of the Holy Temple in Jerusalem by the Babylonians, and the enslavement of the Israelites by their captors, the prophet Jeremiah—never before known for his hopefulness or optimism—quite suddenly began to prophesy that one day the Jews, then being led to Babylon as slaves, would return and rebuild their homeland amid songs of cheer and mirth.

His prophecy came true, and the Jews were permitted to return home after less than a century in exile.

And then in the year 70, the second Holy Temple was destroyed and again the Jews were exiled, this time by the Romans. That exile was to last nearly two thousand years, until the reestablishment of Israel in the year 1948.

The same words that Jeremiah proclaimed are now sung lustily and hopefully at almost every Jewish wedding. They are worth repeating:

> Again shall be heard in this place... in the towns of Judah and the streets of Jerusalem... the sound of mirth and gladness, the voice of bridegroom and bride.

Glossary

Agunah (Agunot, pl) — A woman in limbo: her marriage is over, but she does not have a legal religious divorce, and is unable to marry

Ahavah — Love

Arusah — A betrothed woman

Ashkenazic — The traditions of Jews from central and eastern Europe (as compared with Jews from Mediterranean basin who are known as Sephardic)

BCE — Before the common era

Bedeken — "Covering up" the bride with a veil by the groom, just before the wedding ceremony

Bet din — Jewish religious court

CE — Common era

Chatan (or Chasin) — Bridegroom

Chibur — Combining, joining, sexual intercourse

Chilul Hashem — Disgracing God's name

Chupah — Wedding canopy

Davka — Just because!

E'deem — Witnesses

Erusin — Betrothal, or the first half of the wedding ceremony; in Israel today it means an engagement

Eshet Ish — Married woman

Etrog — Citron, used during the Sukkot holiday service.

Ezer — Companion, helper

Family Purity — Judaism's laws of purity surrounding a woman's monthly period.

Gematriah — Numerology of Hebrew letters, giving Hebrew words mystical interpretations

Ger — A convert to Judaism. *Ger Tsedek* is a convert who became Jewish out of religious reasons

Gerusha — Divorcee

Get — Jewish religious divorce

Gilui Arayot "Uncovering nakedness" — a euphemism for proscribed sexual acts

G'yoret — Woman convert to Judaism

Hachnasat Kalah — Escorting the bride to the wedding; also, a fund to help poor would-be brides

Halachah — Jewish religious law based on Talmudic interpretation of the Bible

Hefker — Ownerless property, or unbridled lust; chaos

Herem — Excommunication

Kalah — Bride

Kasher (or Kosher) — Religiously pure and acceptable

Ketubah — Marriage contract

Kiddush — The blessing offered before the Sabbath meal

Kiddush Hashem — Sanctification of God's name; used also to signify avoidance of defaming God

Kiddushin — Marriage; sanctity; the part of wedding ceremony preceding concluding *nisu'in* section

Kittel — White, unadorned gown worn by some Orthodox grooms at weddings

Kohelet — Ecclesiastes

Kohen — A priestly member of the Jewish community

Lag B'Omer — The 33rd day of the counting of Omer, when weddings may not be held during the period from Passover to *Shavuot*, very popular wedding day in modern Israel

Mamzer — Bastard offspring of adulterous or incestuous union

Mikvah — Ritual pool used for purification

Mitzvah — Good deed, or commandment with religious overtones

Mohar — Cash gift promised by groom to bride in marriage contract

Mored (moredet, fem.) — One who refuses to obey marital obligations

Nadden — Dowry

Niddah — Menstruating woman

Nisu'in — Nuptials

Onah — Obligation, referring to husband's duty to maintain regular marital relations with wife

P'rutah — Smallest denomiation coin

Pilegesh — Concubine

Seder — Passover ritual meal and service

Sefer — Torah Scroll of the Torah (*Pentateuch*)

Sephardim — Jews who originated in Spain and Portugal, and later lived in nearby and distant lands

Shadchan — Matchmaker

Shalom Bayit — Peaceful household

Sheva Brachot — Seven marriage blessings first recited under the *chupah*

Shidduch — A marital match

Taba'at — A ring

Taharat hamishpachah — Family purity

Te'naim — Engagement contract

Torah — The five books of Moses; one-third of the Hebrew Bible. Also used to encompass the concepts of Judaism

Yediah — Knowing, referring to carnal knowledge

Yichud — Togetherness (when bridal couple is momentarily alone right after wedding ceremony)

Yichus — Pedigree, genealogy

Zivig — Heaven-guided marital partner

Zonah — Prostitute; woman who may not for religious reasons marry a kohen

Bibliography

Baron, Joseph L., *A Treasury of Jewish Quotations*. New York, Crown, 1956.

Brav, Stanley R., Ed., *Marriage and the Jewish Tradition*. New York, Philosophical Library, 1951.

Breuer, Joseph, *The Jewish Marriage*. New York, Philipp Felheim, 1956.

Diamant, Anita, *The New Jewish Wedding*. New York, Summit Books, 1985.

Diament, Carol, Ed., *Jewish Marital Status*. Northvale, N.J., Jason Aronson, Inc., 1989.

Drazin, Nathan., *Marriage Made in Heaven*. London, Abelard-Schuman, 1958.

Epstein, M.L., *Marriage Laws in the Bible and Talmud*. Cambridge, Mass., Harvard University Press, 1942.

Epstein, M.L., *Sex Laws and Customs in Judaism*. New York, Bloch Publishing Co., 1948.

Feldman, Aharon., *The River, the Kettle, and the Bird*. Jerusalem, Feldheim, 1989.

Geffen, Rela M., Ed., *Celebration and Renewal*. Philadelphia, Jewish Publication Society, 1993.

Gettlesohn, Roland B., *My Beloved Is Mine*. New York, Union of American Hebrew Congregations, 1969.

Gold, Michael, *And Hannah Wept*. Philadelphia, Jewish Publication Society, 1988.

Goldstein, Sidney E., *Meaning of Marriage and Foundations of the Family*. New York, Bloch Publishing Co., 1942.

Goodman, Philip and Hanna, *The Jewish Marriage Anthology*. Philadephia, Jewish Publication Society, 1965.

Gordis, Robert, *Love and Sex*. New York, Farrar Straus & Giroux, 1978.

Himelstein, Shmuel, *The Jewish Primer*. New York, Facts on File, 1990.

Jacobs, Louis, *What Does Judaism Say About...?* Jerusalem, Keter, 1973.

Kaplan, Aryeh, *Made in Heaven*. New York, Moznaim Publishing Corp., 1983.

Kaufman, Michael, *Love, Marriage and Family in Jewish Law and Tradition*. Northvale, N.J., Jason Aronson, 1992.

Lamm, Maurice, *The Jewish Way in Love and Marriage*. San Francisco, Haper & Row, 1980.

Montefiore, C.G., Loewe, H., Eds., *A Rabbinic Anthology*. New York, Schocken Books, 1974.

Neusner, Jacob, *The Enchantments of Judaism*. New York, Basic Books, 1987.

Rosten, Leo, *Treasury of Jewish Quotations*. New York, McGraw-Hill, 1972.

Routtenberg, Lilly S., Seldin, Ruth R., *Jewish Wedding Book*. New York, Harper & Row, 1967.

Schauss, Hayyim, *The Lifetime of a Jew*. New York, Union of American Hebrew Congregations, 1950.

Schneid, Hayyim, Ed., *Marriage*. Philadelphia, Jewish Publication Society, 1973.

Schwarts, Gwen Gibson, Wyden, Barbara, *The Jewish Wife*. New York, Peter H. Wyden, 1969.

Index

JUDAICA from Hippocrene . . .

THE JEWISH PEOPLE'S ALMANAC
Revised Edition
David C. Gross

The revised edition of a perennial favorite, a compendium of little-known facts and illuminating insights on the history of the Jewish people. Humor, anecdote, and historical fact all have their place in this treasury of Jewish lore.

"Wonderful stories abound." —*Publishers Weekly*
"Laugh, enjoy, and learn." —*Jewish Chronicle*
596 pages • 6 x 9 • 0-7818-0288-1 • $16.95pb

CHOOSING JUDAISM
Lydia Kukoff

This book is designed for those who have already come to Judaism through conversion as well as for those considering it.
"Interesting and touching, splendid advice."
—*Jewish News*
152 pages • 5 ½ x 8 ¼ • 0-87052-070-9 • $7.95pb